Taste of America

Favorite Recipes from Across the USA

Betty Evans

Gulf Publishing Company
Houston, Texas

For three steadfast friends who, filled with American spirit, have contributed boundless inspiration to my life: Joan Clark, Judy Patten, and Joanne Purpus.

Taste of America

Favorite Recipes from Across the USA

Gulf Publishing Company
Book Division
P.O. Box 2608 • Houston, Texas 77252-2608

10 9 8 7 6 5 4 3 2 1

Library of Congress Cataloging-in-Publication Data
Evans, Betty
Taste of America : favorite recipes from across the USA / Betty Evans
p. cm.
Includes index.
ISBN 0-88415-233-2 (alk. paper)
1. Cookery, American. I. Title.
TX715.E88145 1999
641.5973—dc21 98-51764
CIP

Printed in Hong Kong

Photography by Mary Herrmann
Food styling by Kat Hughes
Cover design by Laura A. Dion
Book design by Roxann L. Combs

Contents

Acknowledgments

Thanks to my husband Gordon and our three children, Bob, Suzanne, and Jeanne, for sharing trips in our country. The memories of these adventures were an inspiration for this book.

Always thanks to Steve Hoffmann for his assistance with my computer education and his unique, careful, and inquisitive proofreading.

My appreciation to Kelly D. Perkins, editor, for her special care and originality in preparing *Taste of America*.

Preface

How can one best explain the taste of America? Our nation is the home to more diverse citizens than any other country in the world. In our own unique manner, we are united in a singular style of national cuisine defined by tradition and daring inventions. The recipes contained in this cookbook offer a reflective culinary sampling.

Colonists carried their handwritten recipes from their homelands, finding upon arrival in America that they would need to modify traditional recipes because of the limitations of ingredients and unfamiliar foods in this brave new world. Americans, imbued with inventive Yankee spirit, were always open to spirited change. Today, from sea to shining sea our land offers a lavish abundance of food. Farmer's markets thrive in every state. In many cases they support the small American farmer. For our picnics, holiday gatherings, church suppers, birthday parties, and family dinners, the inventive American cook creates tempting foods for all of us. It is my wholehearted hope that these American recipes might create inspiration for all our happy celebrations.

Betty Evans
Hermosa Beach, California

Beverages

Massachusetts

Cranberries have also been called "bounce berries" because ripe cranberries will bounce.

New Hampshire

This cider may also be served cool with ice cubes in the summer.

Cranberry Cape Codder

Cranberry juice is refreshing and a beautiful color. At the summer homes on Cape Cod, it is often served with vodka for a cooling summer drink.

1 JIGGER (1¼ OUNCES) VODKA
2 JIGGERS CRANBERRY JUICE
ICE CUBES
1 CUP CLUB SODA (OPTIONAL)

For a "short" drink, the vodka and juice are simply poured over ice cubes. For a "tall," follow the same procedure, adding the soda and giving a stir. Serves 1.

Mulled New England Cider

Because of the many apple orchards in New England, drinks made with apple cider are local favorites.

1 QUART BOTTLED APPLE CIDER
½ CUP LIGHT BROWN SUGAR
2 WHOLE CLOVES
1 CINNAMON STICK

Mix ingredients together. Simmer for 10 minutes. Strain and serve in mugs. This will serve 4.

Philadelphia Winter Punch

Philadelphia has a reputation for punches. Some of the recipes from the time of the founding of our country are very strong and create a very sweet, heady mixture. This lovely punch has replaced older recipes and is perfect for winter parties.

- 4 ORANGES (ANY VARIETY)
- 1 CUP SUGAR
- 1 QUART DRY WHITE WINE

Slice oranges crossways into 8 or 9 flat slices (about ⅓ inch thick) and lay them in a baking pan in one layer. Bake at 300° just until they turn light brown. Remove oranges and place in a stainless steel bowl. Cover with sugar and 2 cups of the wine. Stir well, cover, and keep in a cool place for 24 hours. To serve, strain the mixture, pressing orange slices to release the juice. Add the remaining wine. Heat mixture in a pan. Simmer for 2 minutes. Pour into goblets (if desired, add a piece of orange rind retrieved from the strainer). This will serve 4 generously but can be easily doubled or tripled as needed.

Pennsylvania

In colonial days, punch was served in taverns and was a favorite at political gatherings.

Kentucky

Historically, mint juleps were often sipped in the morning because they were thought to have medicinal properties. They were called a demulcent, which simply means a liquid used to soothe inflamed surfaces.

For a perfect presentation, juleps should be served in silver cups.

Mint Julep

To hold a frosted silver cup in your hand and find your senses aroused by this mint and bourbon mélange certainly makes for a rhapsodic moment. Mint juleps are traditionally served at the Kentucky Derby and Churchill Downs.

For each drink you will need:

- 6 tender fresh mint leaves
- 1 tablespoon confectioners' sugar
- 1 tablespoon cold water
- crushed ice
- 4 ounces Kentucky bourbon

If you do not own a silver mint julep cup, you may use any 8-ounce cup. Place the mint, sugar, and water in the cup. Using a bar muddler or wooden spoon, gently crush the mint. Stir until sugar dissolves. Add crushed ice and then the bourbon. Stir with a long-handled spoon. Place in the refrigerator for 20 minutes for the glass to frost. Serve with a long straw and a sprig of mint on top. Hold the glass with a cocktail napkin when serving it so your hand will not disturb the frost.

Southern Summer Lemonade

Driving down Southern roads in the summer in an air-conditioned car can be a comfortable enough experience. However, the minute you open the door and step out into the real weather, it is sort of like a hot blast furnace exploding all over you. As you drive, you will see people sitting in chairs on their spacious front porches with portable fans, drinking lemonade. This is a way to keep cool and relaxed. Lemonade is very much an American drink and one of our finest. Of course, you can simply buy a can of frozen concentrated lemonade, but it will never compare with the taste of freshly made.

- 2 FRESH LEMONS (FOR ABOUT ⅓ CUP JUICE)
- ¾ CUP SUGAR
- 1 QUART WATER
- SPRIGS OF MINT
- ICE CUBES

Squeeze lemons; add sugar, water, and mint to lemon juice. Shake well and refrigerate for flavors to mellow (½ to 6 hours). Pour over ice cubes and serve. This will make 4 large glasses.

Alabama

If desired, a few strips of lemon peel may be added to the lemon juice for a more intense flavor.

Washington

Sometimes a dab of whipped cream is added to the hot cocoa instead of marshmallows.

Oregon

To make attractive ice molds for punch, pour water into a shapely 2–3 cup Jell-O mold. Freeze. To use, unmold and place in the punch bowl.

Seattle Hot Cocoa

Hot cocoa is America's favorite childhood drink, which is not to say that adults, teenagers, and the elderly do not also enjoy cocoa. One of the most pleasant places in the nation to savor hot cocoa is a Seattle cafe overlooking the Puget Sound on a misty day.

- ¼ CUP DRY COCOA
- ½ CUP SUGAR
- ½ CUP WATER
- DASH VANILLA (OPTIONAL)
- 1 QUART MILK
- MARSHMALLOWS (OPTIONAL)

Mix cocoa, sugar, and water together in medium saucepan. Simmer for 3 minutes, stirring to blend. Slowly add milk and vanilla. Stir and heat just until hot—do not boil. Pour into 6 mugs, topping each with marshmallows if desired.

Oregon Celebration Raspberry Punch

Raspberries grow abundantly in Oregon's climate. This punch is popular for weddings and other celebrations.

- 1–2 CUPS FRESH RASPBERRIES (OR 1 10-OUNCE PACKAGE FROZEN)
- 1 BOTTLE CHAMPAGNE, CHILLED
- 1 FIFTH DRY WHITE WINE, CHILLED

Wash fresh raspberries gently and pat dry. If frozen, thaw. Combine with champagne and wine in a glass punch bowl. This will serve 6–8.

Summer Arkansas Iced Tea

Arkansas

Foreign visitors are always curious about the popularity of iced tea in our nation. In other countries, it is just not served.

This is the most popular beverage in Arkansas homes, restaurants, and small cafes. It quenches thirst and is most refreshing.

1½ TEASPOONS TEA (YOUR CHOICE) TO EACH CUP OF WATER
SUGAR TO TASTE
ICE CUBES
LEMON SLICES
MINT SPRIGS (OPTIONAL)

Prepare in a teapot by putting the tea in the teapot and then pouring boiling water into it. Cover and let steep for 3–5 minutes. Pour through strainer into pitcher. Add sugar and stir to mix. Refrigerate until needed. Serve in tall glasses over ice cubes, with lemon slices and a sprig of mint if desired.

Arizona Margaritas

Arizona

Margaritas are refreshing and perfect with Southwest Mexican food.

The darling of Southwestern drinks is the classic Mexican margarita. Many restaurants offer the double in big bubble glasses.

LIME WEDGE
SALT
1½ OUNCES TEQUILA
¾ OUNCE ORANGE LIQUEUR (TRIPLE SEC OR OTHER)
1½ TABLESPOONS LIME JUICE (FRESH PREFERRED)
CRUSHED ICE

California

Irish coffee was created by Joe Sheridan in 1949 at the Shannon Airport in Ireland for passengers who were cold and in need of a hot drink.

Take the lime wedge and rub around the rim of a medium-sized glass or goblet. Place a layer of salt on a saucer. Rub the rim in salt to coat edge. In a separate container, combine tequila, orange liqueur, and lime juice. Mix well. Add ice. Mix or shake to combine ingredients. Pour into glass. This will make 1 margarita.

San Francisco Irish Coffee

The Buena Vista is a bar and restaurant located at the corner of Hyde and Beach streets in San Francisco. This is where Irish coffee was first served in California. Stanton Delaplane, a travel writer, brought this recipe to the Buena Vista from Ireland's Shannon Airport. Irish coffee makes a pleasant winter dessert.

- 1 JIGGER (1¼ OUNCES) IRISH WHISKEY
- 2 SUGAR CUBES
- STRONG, HOT COFFEE
- SLIGHTLY SWEETENED WHIPPING CREAM

Pour whiskey into a warmed glass. Add sugar cubes, followed by hot coffee. It is advisable to place a metal spoon in the glass to avoid possible breakage (the spoon will attract the heat). Stir whiskey, sugar, and coffee together. I use a spoon to gently float the cream on top of the coffee. You do not want the cream to blend with the coffee, as the joy of an Irish coffee is to sip the coffee through the cool, white cream. Use only real whipping cream. It should be whipped just until thick, but not stiff. Serves 1.

Mike's Mai Tai

Hawaii

It is most pleasant to lounge on a shaded terrace in the Hawaiian Islands, sipping a cool tropical drink. This drink is an Island favorite from Mike Purpus, a world-famous surfer who has participated in many Hawaiian surfing competitions. Here is Mike's original mai tai recipe.

- 1 JIGGER (1¼ OUNCES) WHITE RUM
- 2 OUNCES ORANGE JUICE
- 2 OUNCES PINEAPPLE JUICE
- 1½ OUNCES COCONUT SYRUP
- CRUSHED ICE
- 1 JIGGER "151" STRONG DARK RUM
- ½ OUNCE CHERRY-FLAVORED BRANDY
- SPLASH OF GRENADINE SYRUP

Mix white rum, juices, and coconut syrup together. Fill a 10- to 12-ounce tulip glass with crushed ice. Pour the rum/juice mixture over the ice. Add the jigger of "151" on top. Float the cherry-flavored brandy on top, with a splash of grenadine. This will make 1 drink.

Hawaiian cocktails are often garnished with an orchid or some other exotic flower and served with macadamia nuts.

See photo on p. 1.

Soups,
Salads,
Sauces,
Dips,
&
Other
Appetizers

New Mexico

On one of those blistering New Mexico summer days, Georgia might have preferred this soup cold. To serve it that way, simply cool soup and refrigerate. Stir before serving.

Georgia O'Keeffe Watercress Soup

In the small town of Abiquiu, in northern New Mexico, Georgia O'Keeffe lived and painted many of her famous desert landscape works, inspired by the dramatic mountains, rocks, and sky of the surrounding countryside. O'Keeffe's cooking was simple and earthy, in keeping with her character, and she enjoyed watercress soup. Here is a version I think this great American woman might have liked very much.

- 1 POUND WHITE ROSE OR RED POTATOES, PEELED AND SLICED
- 4 CUPS WATER
- 1 MEDIUM WHITE ONION, PEELED AND DICED
- SALT AND PEPPER TO TASTE
- 1 BUNCH WATERCRESS
- 1 CUP MILK OR HALF-AND-HALF
- ¼ CUP DRY WHITE WINE (OPTIONAL)

Place the potatoes, water, onion, salt, and pepper in a soup pot. Cover and simmer for about 40 minutes until the potatoes are very tender. While the potatoes are simmering, remove and discard about 1 inch of the watercress stems. Wash well. Cut across the bunch of watercress with a knife or scissors until the watercress is in 1-inch lengths. When the potatoes are done, remove from heat and break them up with a fork or potato masher, just until they are crumbly (do not use a blender or food processor, as you do not want a mush). Add watercress to soup and cook over low flame for 5 minutes. Add milk or half-and-half and then wine (if used). Stir to blend and heat just to serving temperature. Do not boil. This will serve 5.

Senate Bean Soup

Washington, D.C.

Senate Bean Soup is one of the culinary pleasures of the United States Capitol Senate Restaurant in Washington, D.C. Anyone can dine in this Capitol restaurant, but you do need to let your senator know ahead of time. My California senator, Dianne Feinstein, helped me obtain some of the history of this famed American soup. Its origin is popularly attributed to Senator Fred Thomas Dubois of Idaho, who served in the Senate from 1901 to 1907. While he was chairman of the committee that supervised the restaurant, he gaveled through a resolution requiring that bean soup be on the menu every day.

- 2 pounds small Michigan navy beans (or other)
- 4 quarts hot water
- 1½ smoked ham hocks
- 1 onion, chopped
- 2 tablespoons butter
- Salt and pepper to taste

Wash the beans and place in a pot of hot water. Add ham hocks and boil slowly for approximately 3½ hours, covered. Stir now and then. Take ham hocks from pot and remove meat. Cut meat in small pieces and return to soup. Braise onion in butter until light brown, and then add to soup. Season to taste with salt and pepper. This will make 8 servings.

In some versions of this soup, 1 cup of mashed potatoes is stirred in during the last hour of cooking.

Hawaii

Some island residents peel Maui onions and eat them raw, like apples.

Maui Onion Soup

The onions of Maui are very sweet and tender. Thinly sliced onion rings are added to salads and sandwiches, and are used for garnishes. An onion soup prepared with these special onions tastes especially delicious.

- 4 TABLESPOONS BUTTER
- 2 TABLESPOONS PEANUT OR SESAME OIL
- 6 MEDIUM MAUI ONIONS OR OTHER SWEET ONIONS, SLICED THINLY
- SALT AND PEPPER TO TASTE
- 1 TABLESPOON FLOUR
- 2 QUARTS CHICKEN BROTH (MAY BE HOMEMADE OR CANNED)
- 1 CUP DRY WHITE WINE
- SOY SAUCE FOR GARNISH

Heat butter and oil in soup pot. Add sliced onions. Over a low flame, stir-fry until onions are limp but not brown. Cover and cook over low flame for 15 minutes, giving a stir now and then. Uncover. Stir in salt, pepper, and flour. Add broth and wine. Simmer over a low flame, uncovered, for 40 minutes.

This will serve 6. Add a few drops of soy sauce to each bowl for an island touch.

New Mexico Albondigas Soup

Albondigas simply means "little meatballs" in Spanish. In New Mexico, this soup is popular on nippy winter evenings. You can improve it by preparing it ahead of time so the flavors can mellow. Serve it with warm tortillas and a fresh green salad to make a good, comforting dinner.

- 1 TABLESPOON VEGETABLE OIL
- 1 MEDIUM ONION, MINCED
- 1 CLOVE GARLIC, MINCED
- 1 SLICE WHITE BREAD
- 1 EGG, SLIGHTLY BEATEN
- 1 POUND LEAN GROUND BEEF (OR ½ POUND EACH GROUND BEEF AND PORK)
- ½ TEASPOON OREGANO
- ½ CUP WHITE OR YELLOW CORNMEAL
- 1 FRESH GREEN ANAHEIM CHILE, CHOPPED FINELY (OR ¼ CUP CANNED, DICED)
- SALT AND PEPPER TO TASTE
- 1 QUART CHICKEN OR BEEF STOCK (HOMEMADE OR CANNED)
- 1 8-OUNCE CAN TOMATO SAUCE

Heat oil in a frying pan. Lightly brown the onion and garlic. Crumble the bread into the beaten egg. Mix the bread and egg together. Add to meat, along with onion, garlic, oregano, cornmeal, chile, salt, and pepper. Make this mixture into meatballs about the size of walnuts.

Heat the stock with the tomato sauce. Drop the meatballs into the soup and simmer, uncovered, for 25 minutes. To serve, place 3 meatballs in each soup bowl. This will make 6 servings.

New Mexico

If any albondigas are left over, they make good sandwiches.

New York

There are many variations on this salad. Sometimes, a cup of cubed chicken, ham, or baby shrimp is added. For a Middle Eastern flavor, you can add 1 teaspoon curry powder and ½ cup raisins. For a Pacific feeling, try adding some pineapple chunks.

See photo on pp. 10–11.

Waldorf Salad

Waldorf salad is a true American classic, created for the opening of New York's Waldorf Hotel in 1893. Since then, it has come to be one of the nation's favorite salads. My mother made this salad often, and this is her version of it.

- 3 APPLES (RED, GREEN, OR YELLOW)
- 3 TABLESPOONS LEMON JUICE
- 1 CUP DICED CELERY
- ½ CUP COARSELY CHOPPED WALNUTS (CAN BE LIGHTLY TOASTED)
- ½ CUP MAYONNAISE
- 1 TABLESPOON POPPY SEEDS
- LEAVES OF BUTTER OR ICEBERG LETTUCE (WASHED)

Dice the apples. Sprinkle with lemon juice and mix for an even coating. Add remaining ingredients (except lettuce), and blend gently. Serve on lettuce leaves. This will serve 4.

Maryann's Jersey Tomato Salad

My friend Maryann is from New Jersey. She has an Italian mother, an Irish father, and a lovely accent that is an engaging mixture of her Jersey, Irish, and Italian heritage. Maryann enjoys sharing tales of family cooking in New Jersey. One of her favorite dishes is this deceptively simple tomato salad, which is a taste sensation masterpiece of Jersey summer tomatoes.

Summer in New Jersey is one of Maryann's nostalgic memories. There, almost every homeowner with a little patch of green grows lovely Jersey tomatoes. They are big, juicy, and luscious to eat right from the yard. New Jersey residents are so proud of their August tomatoes that it is a common practice to exchange tomatoes with neighbors, friends, and relatives, comparing the tomatoes to determine who grew the best.

3–4 JERSEY TOMATOES
3 TABLESPOONS FRESH BASIL
EXTRA-VIRGIN OLIVE OIL
KOSHER SALT
FRESHLY GROUND PEPPER

Quarter or eighth the tomatoes depending on the size. Place in a large mixing bowl. Sliver or tear fresh basil leaves into the bowl, over the tomatoes. Drizzle olive oil, salt, and pepper to taste over tomatoes. Mix very gently. Jersey tomato salad is best served at room temperature. How many this will serve depends on your appetite for tomatoes! (Fresh vine-ripened tomatoes are the nearest substitute for authentic Jersey tomatoes.)

New Jersey

New Jersey is known as the Garden State. In New Jersey tomatoes are consumed as soon as possible after picking. This is when a tomato is the very best! If you must keep your tomatoes a few days, simply store them in a cool place in your kitchen. Do not refrigerate because this will take away the fresh flavor.

Hawaii

Although most identify the macadamia nut with Hawaii, it actually originated in Australia. The seeds were brought to Hawaii from Queensland in 1882. Hawaii is the largest producer in the world of this "king of the nuts."

Hanalei Bay Chicken Salad

Hanalei Bay is one of the treasures of Kauai. The beautiful curving bay, fringed with palm trees, is an ideal spot for picnics and a scene to remain in visitors' island memories. Our friends Marilyn and Ed moved there from Hermosa Beach, California, many years ago. When we visited them, they had a picnic lunch all prepared. We sat on the warm sand by the bay and munched on this pleasant chicken salad. Marilyn had also brought freshly baked banana bread, which tasted utterly perfect with our lunch.

- 2 CUPS COOKED AND DICED CHICKEN BREAST
- 1 8¼-OUNCE CAN PINEAPPLE CHUNKS, DRAINED, OR 1 CUP FRESH PINEAPPLE CHUNKS
- 1 CUP TRIMMED CELERY, CUT IN SMALL DICES
- ¼ CUP MACADAMIA NUTS OR PEANUTS, COARSELY CHOPPED
- 1 TEASPOON CURRY POWDER
- SALT AND PEPPER TO TASTE
- ¼ CUP MAYONNAISE OR PLAIN YOGURT
- FRESH CILANTRO LEAVES (OPTIONAL)

Combine all the ingredients (except cilantro) in a bowl. Mix together and refrigerate. This may be prepared a day ahead. Garnish with fresh cilantro leaves if desired. This salad will serve 4.

Harlem Barbecue Sauce for an Artist's Party

New York

When we lived in New York, some of my husband's colleagues from the Art Students League would get together for potluck dinners. The food contributions would be laid out on a big studio table covered with brightly colored construction paper. We ate from paper plates, and everyone had a great time. One of the best dishes anyone ever brought was a platter of chicken covered with this splendid, tangy sauce.

- ½ cup butter
- 1 medium onion, minced
- 2 cloves garlic, minced
- 1 teaspoon mustard
- ½ teaspoon cayenne
- 1 teaspoon Tabasco or other hot sauce
- 2 tablespoons ketchup
- 2 tablespoons lemon juice
- 2 tablespoons red or white wine vinegar
- 1 8-ounce can tomato sauce
- 2 tablespoons finely chopped parsley
- Salt and pepper to taste

Melt butter in a saucepan. Lightly cook onion and garlic in butter just until limp (not browned). Add remaining ingredients and cook over a low flame for 10 minutes. This will make enough to "sauce" 2 chickens, 8 pork chops, or 6 pounds of spareribs, cooked as desired.

In cooking lingo, "dry rub" means the spices are rubbed into the food, and "wet rub" means the food is immersed in a marinade.

Connecticut

If you have some of this dip left over, you can use it as a stuffing for chiles rellenos. It is a most tasty combination.

Paula's Mystic Hot Crab Dip

Mystic, a historic seaport in Connecticut, was a nineteenth-century shipbuilding and whaling town. Seamen left from there on lengthy voyages to gather whale oil from every sea. Today, Mystic is filled with tourists, who can board the celebrated old sailing ships, have fresh seafood meals, and shop for souvenirs and antiques. My friend Joan's daughter, Paula, married a man from Mystic, and now she and her family live in this fascinating town. Paula sent me this delicious recipe for the local hot crab dip. Many New England inns and taverns offer this sort of thing as an appetizer to guests awaiting dinner.

- 1 8-ounce package cream cheese, at room temperature
- 1 6-ounce can good-quality crabmeat, drained (or 1 cup fresh or imitation crabmeat)
- 1 tablespoon horseradish
- 2 tablespoons milk
- 2 tablespoons finely chopped white onion or 2 minced green onions
- Freshly ground black pepper to taste
- 2 tablespoons bread crumbs
- Paprika for garnish

Combine all ingredients except bread crumbs and paprika. Blend well and place in a small ovenproof dish. Sprinkle with bread crumbs and paprika. Bake at 350° for 20 minutes. This makes about 2 cups. Serve with crackers.

Las Vegas Shrimp Cocktail

The first time I went to Las Vegas countless years ago, I was on the way to Utah to visit relatives. This was our overnight stay on the road to Salt Lake City. My husband and I both had Mormon great-grandfathers, and we have always been curious—could they have known each other? My relative was from Scotland and Gordon's from Wales.

It was almost dinnertime, and we wandered into a casino. A food counter was serving shrimp cocktails for only ten cents. The pale pink shrimp were in little glass bowls covered with a reddish sauce. I ordered two cocktails. They were cool and refreshing after the warm, monotonous drive. It occurred to me that it was a rather remarkable experience to nibble these pretty gems from the sea in the midst of a dry Nevada desert. The curious city of Las Vegas is an American novelty, and shrimp cocktails have been a traditional food offering here almost since the city's founding. Shrimp cocktails are not only popular in Las Vegas; almost every restaurant menu in our country has a place for a shrimp cocktail.

- 1 POUND COOKED AND PEELED SHRIMP, CHILLED
- 3 TABLESPOONS LEMON JUICE

Cocktail Sauce

- ¾ CUP CHILI SAUCE
- ½ CUP KETCHUP
- 1 TABLESPOON FINELY MINCED ONION (CHIVES MAY BE USED)
- 1 TABLESPOON HORSERADISH
- 2 TABLESPOONS FINELY MINCED FRESH CELERY
- SALT AND PEPPER TO TASTE

Mix shrimp and lemon juice together in a bowl and refrigerate. Place all the sauce ingredients in another bowl, blend, and refrigerate. To serve, place shrimp and lemon juice in 4 bowls (for small cocktails). Dribble sauce over top and serve at once.

Nevada

Shrimp are sold both raw and cooked. Raw shrimp should be firm and smell like the sea; if there is an unpleasant odor or squishiness, do not buy them. Cooked shrimp should also be firm with tight shells.

LAGUNA
OCEANSIDE
SAN DIEGO

Side Dishes

Nebraska

This dish can be prepared ahead and refrigerated if desired; if you choose this method, add an extra 15–20 minutes for baking.

Nebraska Fourth of July Macaroni & Cheese

In Nebraska, spirited picnics are part of the Cornhusker State's Fourth of July celebrations. Long tables are set out in local parks for the jubilant feasts. Casseroles of macaroni and cheese are plentiful, as this dish is a favorite food for our great national holiday.

- ½ POUND ELBOW MACARONI
- WATER
- SALT (FOR WATER)
- 4 TABLESPOONS BUTTER
- 4 TABLESPOONS FLOUR
- 2 CUPS MILK
- 1 GREEN ONION, MINCED
- SALT AND PEPPER TO TASTE
- 2 CUPS GRATED SHARP CHEDDAR CHEESE
- BUTTER (FOR GREASING DISH)
- 1–2 TABLESPOONS BREAD CRUMBS
- MINCED PARSLEY AND PAPRIKA FOR GARNISH

Cook the macaroni in rapidly boiling salted water until tender but not mushy. Drain and set aside while you make the sauce. Melt the butter in a heavy saucepan. Add the flour. For 2–3 minutes, blend well and cook together for a minute. Stir in the milk, onion, salt, and pepper. Cook over a low flame for 2–3 minutes, stirring to make a smooth mixture. Blend in and melt the grated cheese as the sauce is cooking. When the sauce has thickened (2–3 minutes), mix with the macaroni. Place in a buttered 2- to 3-quart attractive baking dish and sprinkle the bread crumbs over the top. Bake at 350° for 20–25 minutes until bubbly and light brown on top. Sprinkle with parsley and paprika. This will serve 4.

California Mission Days Green Chile Rice

The missions founded by Father Serra in Carmel in 1770 are some of the main tourist attractions of California. They stretch from San Diego to San Rafael—twenty-two of them in all. Today, most are open to visitors, with displays and exhibits about California mission life. Often, they host demonstrations of various crafts from mission times. All the missions had gardens for growing the produce needed to feed the many people who worked there. Rice was one of the popular dishes of mission cuisine, and this blend of rice with green chiles is one of my favorite recipes.

- 3 CUPS COOKED RICE (1 CUP BEFORE COOKING)
- 1 TEASPOON CHILI POWDER
- 1 TEASPOON CUMIN SEED OR CUMIN POWDER (OPTIONAL)
- 1 TEASPOON SALT
- 2 CUPS SOUR CREAM
- OIL (FOR BAKING DISH)
- 1 6-OUNCE CAN GREEN CHILES (OR 4 FRESH, PEELED CHILES), MINCED
- 2 CUPS GRATED MONTEREY JACK OR CHEDDAR CHEESE
- CILANTRO, TOMATO SLICES, OR OLIVES FOR GARNISH (OPTIONAL)

Cook rice by your favorite method. Cool slightly. Add chili powder, cumin, and salt. Mix in sour cream and stir well. Lightly oil a 1½-quart baking dish. Layer half the rice mixture, then half the green chiles, and then half the cheese. Repeat, ending with the cheese. Bake in a 350° oven for 25 minutes, uncovered. Garnish if desired with fresh cilantro, sliced tomatoes, or a few sliced olives. This will serve 6.

California

You can make a main dish of this classic by adding 1–2 cups cooked chicken pieces, bay shrimp, or shredded pork. It is a perfect potluck contribution and goes well as a side dish for barbecue dinners.

See photo on pp. 22–23.

Tennessee

It is a Southern tradition on New Year's to serve collards for health and Hoppin' John for money. They are served side by side for New Year's festivities.

Hoppin' John

There is a passage in Tennessee Williams's *Cat on a Hot Tin Roof* in which Big Mama feels encouraged about the health of Big Daddy because he has eaten two portions of Hoppin' John. Southern legends say Hoppin' John was a lame plantation cook who hopped on one leg while serving this dish. If leftovers are served, they are called Skipping Jenny, after his wife who skipped. In some Southern households, children like to get into a playful game of hopping once around the table before they sit down to eat. This is a large recipe, making plenty for big daddies. It freezes well and is a good leftover.

- 1 POUND DRIED BLACK-EYED PEAS
- 1 ONION, PEELED AND CHOPPED
- WATER
- ½ POUND BACON SLICES
- SALT AND PEPPER TO TASTE
- 2 CUPS LONG-GRAIN RICE, UNCOOKED
- HOT SAUCE (OPTIONAL)

Place the peas and chopped onion in a large, deep, heavy pot. Cover with water. You will need enough water for the peas to expand. Add the bacon, and season with salt and pepper. Cover and simmer until barely tender, about 1 hour.

Uncover and add more water, if needed; you will need 4 cups of liquid to cook the rice. Add rice and simmer covered for about 30 minutes. The rice and peas should not be mushy. Each serving should have a slice of bacon. Serve with hot sauce if desired. This makes about 6 servings.

South Carolina Baked Cheese Grits

Visitors to the South like to joke about grits, a staple served at breakfast, lunch, and dinner. Many servicemen who were stationed in the South may have memories of unattractive mess-hall grits, but when grits are properly prepared (which is simple), they are most satisfying and pleasant. They can be turned into a lovely side dish to accompany any food. Southern chefs these days are having fun adding mushrooms, turnip greens, or cheeses to their grits. This recipe is a popular one.

- 3 CUPS WATER
- ½ TEASPOON SALT
- ¾ CUP QUICK-COOKING GRITS
- 1 CUP MILK
- 1 EGG, BEATEN
- 4 GREEN ONION TOPS, THINLY SLICED CROSSWAYS
- 1½ CUPS GRATED CHEDDAR CHEESE
- 1 TEASPOON HOT PEPPER SAUCE (OPTIONAL)
- 2 TABLESPOONS BUTTER, AT ROOM TEMPERATURE
- GREASE (FOR BAKING DISH)

Heat water and salt to boiling. Slowly stir in the grits. Cover pan and cook over low heat for 6 minutes, stirring now and then so grits do not stick to pan. In a separate bowl, mix together remaining ingredients except grease. Remove grits from pan and blend well with this mixture. Place all in a greased 1½- or 2-quart baking dish, and bake uncovered at 350° for 20 minutes. This will serve 4.

South Carolina

Native Americans taught the settlers how to grind corn. (Grits are simply hulled, coarse ground corn.) In America, corn is our only native grain.

Massachusetts

Sugar cane was shipped from the West Indies into Boston Harbor to be made into molasses. It was also distilled into rum. When the British added a cane tax, the undaunted Massachusetts men smuggled this necessary ingredient onto land.

Boston Baked Beans

The Pilgrims baked their Sunday beans on Saturday because of the religious mandate that dictated Sunday as a day of rest. They baked them overnight in brick ovens, but with today's modern stoves, baked beans can easily be prepared in 5 hours. Baking beans is a wonderful kitchen experience, as appetizing scents fill the house. If you wish, you can bake brown bread at the same time, just as the efficient New England ladies did.

- 2 CUPS (1 POUND) SMALL WHITE DRIED BEANS
- 4 QUARTS WATER
- 1 TEASPOON SALT
- ½ POUND SALT PORK
- 1 TEASPOON DRY MUSTARD OR 2 TEASPOONS DIJON-STYLE MUSTARD
- ⅓ CUP DARK BROWN SUGAR
- ¼ CUP MOLASSES
- 1 ONION, DICED
- SALT AND PEPPER TO TASTE

New research indicates that soaking beans is not necessary. The cooking time may be a little longer as a consequence, but the flavor will be more intense.

Place the beans in a large pot. Cover with water and salt. Cover and simmer until just barely tender, about 1 hour. (Old purists say "until you can blow away the skins," which the eminent cookbook writer Fanny Farmer explains thusly: "Taking a few beans on the tip of a spoon, blow on them; the skins will burst if sufficiently cooked. Beans thus tested must of course be thrown away." Other Boston writers simply say to cook until the bean skins wrinkle and crack.)

Drain the beans, reserving the liquid. Cut slits in the pork rind to prevent it from curling. Place the pork in a bean pot (or a 5–6 quart heavy casserole dish with a tight lid) and cover with 3 quarts of the reserved liquid; stir in mustard, brown sugar, molasses, onion, salt, and pepper. Add beans, placing the salt pork deep in the center. Bake at 300°, covered, for 3 hours, stirring now and then and adding additional reserved bean liquid as necessary.

Remove cover and bring salt pork to the top to brown. Cook an additional hour. This will serve 8.

Chicago Polish Asparagus

Illinois

Chicago, famed as the Windy City, has the largest Polish population of any city in the world, including cities in Poland. Polish cooking is hearty and flavorful. Poland and Chicago both have severe winters, and the coming of spring is a joyous event. Asparagus is a part of the Polish springtime celebration. This recipe is easy and brings out the best of the fresh, pert flavor of asparagus.

- 3 POUNDS FRESH THIN TO MEDIUM ASPARAGUS STALKS
- WATER
- ¼ CUP (½ STICK) BUTTER
- 5 TABLESPOONS WHITE BREAD CRUMBS
- SALT AND PEPPER TO TASTE
- PINCH OF SUGAR

Wash asparagus and discard tough bottom stem. This is easily done by holding the stalk and snapping the top from the bottom; it will break naturally at the right place. Fill a large pot with water and bring to a boil. Add asparagus and boil, uncovered, over a medium flame for about 10 minutes. While asparagus is cooking, melt the butter in a pan, add crumbs and seasonings, and lightly brown. Drain the asparagus immediately and lay on a warm serving platter. Spoon the crumbs over the top. This will serve 6.

For top flavor, asparagus must be kept very fresh. To do this, pretend the asparagus is a bouquet. Place the stems in a jar containing 2 inches of water and cover loosely with plastic wrap. Store in refrigerator.

Main Dishes

Alaska

At the Alaska State Fair, corn on the cob, a big serving of beans, and two paper napkins are the embellishments for this dish.

MEAT

Alaska State Fair Barbecued Spareribs

The annual Alaska State Fair is held in the fertile Matanuska Valley, where cabbages can grow up to seventy pounds in the short summer season. The rugged Chugach Mountain range that rises above the valley gives the whole fair a travel-poster look. As at any state fair, quilts, rabbits, and big zucchini are on display, but do-it-yourself log cabins and fur shoes add a distinctively local touch.

The food is hearty, and barbecued ribs, served fresh off the fire out of a big metal tub, are a favorite. Carefully, you carry your plate over to the "Sluice Box," a Quonset hut with long tables, beer, and a neighborhood Western band. Everyone there is chomping on ribs and having fun.

- 2 TABLESPOONS BUTTER
- 1 ONION, FINELY CHOPPED
- 2 CLOVES GARLIC, MINCED
- ¾ CUP KETCHUP
- ½ CUP WATER
- 1 TEASPOON MUSTARD
- SALT AND PEPPER TO TASTE
- 3–4 POUNDS BEEF OR PORK SPARERIBS

To make the barbecue sauce, melt the butter in a saucepan, add onion and garlic, and cook over medium heat just until limp. Add remaining ingredients through salt and pepper. Stir and simmer, uncovered, for 10 minutes. Barbecue the ribs on a grill over charcoal, basting with sauce.

The ribs may also be baked in the oven: Place ribs on a metal rack over a shallow baking pan (to catch drippings) and bake for 30 minutes at 425°. Pour off fat carefully. Turn down oven to 375° and bake ribs an additional 30 minutes, basting several times with sauce. This will serve 4.

Texas

William Gebhart of New Braunfels, Texas, began packaging a dry blend of chili powder in 1896. He named it Tampico Dust and later changed the name to Eagle. It was a blend of spices including chili pepper, oregano, cumin, and garlic. This easy-to-use powder introduced chili to many parts of our country.

Prize-Winning Texas Chili

The dying words of the American frontier hero Kit Carson were reputedly, "Wish I had time for one more bowl of chili!" Affectionately known as "a bowl of red," chili is a uniquely American dish.

The Texas town of Terlingua is famed worldwide for its serious chili contests. Although I have not entered my own chili recipe there, I have been a judge at local chili cook-offs. This is fun, but I approach it with caution. Once I had to taste sixteen samples. Usually the dishes of chili are scored from 1 to 10, and often there is a tie, and a few must be retasted. Chili should look appetizing and should have a pleasant aroma that appeals to your taste buds. First I look at the chili, which should be served in a sturdy white china bowl. If the chili appears gray and greasy, I immediately give it low marks. The next step is to take a spoonful and slowly roll it around your mouth. This is to capture the flavors before swallowing. Chili texture is important. It should not be soupy. After each taste, I drink a swig of beer to clean my palate. Beer works better for this than soda crackers or bread! In serious contests, ground meat is never used, although it is the main ingredient in "Texas jailhouse chili." Jails in Texas began serving chili to their prisoners in the late 1800s as a way to use inexpensive cuts of meat. The Dallas County jail in the '30s still holds the reputation for the best jailhouse chili ever made.

I have used the following basic recipe for my cooking classes. Individual chili chefs can add more or less of the various ingredients according to their desires.

- 2–3 TABLESPOONS OIL OR LARD
- 1 ONION, CHOPPED
- 1 CLOVE GARLIC, MINCED
- 1 JALAPEÑO PEPPER, FINELY CHOPPED (OPTIONAL)
- 2 POUNDS BEEF (BONELESS CHUCK OR ROUND STEAK) OR BONELESS PORK SHOULDER, CUT INTO ½-INCH CUBES
- 2 TABLESPOONS CHILI POWDER
- 1 TEASPOON DRIED OREGANO (OPTIONAL)
- SALT AND PEPPER TO TASTE
- 1 TABLESPOON GROUND CUMIN
- 1 CUP LIQUID (BEER, RED WINE, TEQUILA, BROTH, ETC.)
- 1 28-OUNCE CAN DICED OR CRUSHED TOMATOES, UNDRAINED
- 1 4-OUNCE CAN DICED GREEN CHILES, DRAINED

Heat the oil or lard in a stew pot. Lightly brown the onion, garlic, and jalapeño pepper in the oil or lard. Remove from pot with a slotted spoon and set aside. Place the meat, chili powder, oregano, salt, pepper, and cumin into pot, and brown lightly, adding more oil if necessary. Return onion, garlic, and jalapeño pepper to pan, along with the liquid, tomatoes, and green chiles. Cover and cook over a low flame for 1 hour and 15 minutes, until the meat is tender, stirring now and then. The chili's flavors will mellow if it is made a day ahead. Serve in bowls to 4.

This recipe may be enlarged for a chili party. If desired, serve with bowls of grated Monterey Jack or cheddar cheese, minced onions, sour cream, finely chopped red or green chiles, olives, or snipped cilantro.

It is believed that chili originated in San Antonio, Texas, among the impoverished. By adding peppers to a small amount of beef, the meal could be enlarged to feed more people. Around 1880, chili stands were set up in the plazas of this city. Soon it became a nightly custom to take an evening stroll and take pleasure in eating a bowl of hot chili.

Oregon

Oregon's blue cheese is famed and flavorful because of the high-quality milk produced in this state. The blue veins are formed by a harmless penicillin mold.

Steaks with Oregon Blue Cheese Topping

Blue cheese salad dressings are popular nationwide, and that is the way most Americans know this cheese. The state of Oregon is a famous blue cheese producer. One of my friends moved from California to Oregon and raves about the quiet and beauty there. The recipe is one she sent to me that uses her adopted state's famous dairy product. The lively flavors taste perfect with steak.

- ¼ CUP BLUE CHEESE, AT ROOM TEMPERATURE
- ¼ CUP SWEET BUTTER (BUTTER WITH NO ADDED SALT), AT ROOM TEMPERATURE
- 1 CLOVE GARLIC, MINCED
- 4 STEAKS (¾–1 POUND EACH; RIB EYE, NEW YORK, OR TOP SIRLOIN)
- SALT AND FRESHLY GROUND PEPPER TO TASTE

Combine cheese, butter, and garlic. Mash into a paste with a fork. Set aside. Sprinkle the steaks with salt and pepper to taste. Preheat your broiler. Broil the first side of the steaks about 2 inches from the heat. (The amount of time will depend on the thickness, but it usually takes about 6 minutes on each side.) Pull out the broiler pan, turn steaks to the second side, and spread the tasty topping over the top surface of each steak. Return to broiler and finish cooking until desired doneness. This will serve 4.

Cathy's Mom's Great Pork & Sauerkraut

My friend Cathy Zadel, who spent her childhood in the small Minnesota town of Sauk Centre, is a most ardent cook. She loves to tell me tales of her mother, who was also a gifted cook and loved to try new recipes. This was a favorite dinner at their home on cold, snowy winter nights.

- 2 POUNDS SAUERKRAUT (REFRIGERATED, BOTTLED, OR CANNED)
- 1 LARGE ONION, CHOPPED
- 6 RED POTATOES, WHOLE IF SMALL OR QUARTERED IF LARGE
- 6 GARLIC CLOVES, PEELED
- 2 TABLESPOONS JUNIPER BERRIES
- 2 TABLESPOONS CARAWAY SEED
- SALT AND PEPPER TO TASTE
- 1 CUP DRY WHITE WINE
- 2 CUPS CHICKEN BROTH
- 1 PORK LOIN ROAST (3–4 POUNDS)

Rinse the sauerkraut well and drain. Put in a 10″ × 14″ roasting pan. Add everything except the roast. Mix together. Place roast in center of pan on top of the sauerkraut. Roast at 325° for 3 hours. Stir sauerkraut around several times and baste pork with pan juices. This will serve 4–6.

Minnesota

The technique of making sauerkraut has not changed since the Roman times (the Romans discovered it in the Orient). Sauerkraut is prepared by first shredding some cabbage. The cabbage is then layered and sprinkled with salt and sometimes juniper berries. This is all placed in a large earthenware container and covered with a weighted lid. It then ferments, creating sauerkraut.

Pennsylvania

Sliced leftover roast works well as the beef for these sandwiches.

Philly Cheese Steak Sandwiches for a Football Party

I have eaten Philly cheese steak sandwiches at fairs in the West and found the dry meats and stale buns not too exciting. This all changed for me when I was at the Pittsburgh airport, changing planes for a flight to Los Angeles. I noticed a line at the Philly cheese steak concession. Suddenly I felt hungry and joined the line. The cook was stirring succulent pieces of finely shaved roast beef on a hot griddle with onions. He asked if I wanted mayo, lettuce, and tomato. Yes, I wanted it all and also a bottle of the local beer. The sandwich was marvelous. The meat and onions were flavorful, and all the ingredients were layered in perfect proportions on an excellent bun. I relished every bite. The homey warmth of this American classic makes it a perfect candidate for a cool-day lunch or light supper.

For each sandwich you will need:

¼ CUP SLICED ONIONS
OIL (FOR THE GRILL)
SEVERAL THIN SLICES OF ROAST BEEF
1 FRESH BUN, TOP AND BOTTOM, OF YOUR CHOICE (USUALLY THESE ARE LONG, ABOUT 7 INCHES, ALTHOUGH HAMBURGER BUNS CAN ALSO BE USED)
CHEESE SLICES (PROVOLONE IS A GOOD CHOICE)
LETTUCE
TOMATO SLICES

Lightly brown sliced onions in a greased frying pan. Add sliced meat and stir until hot. Heat bun just until warm but not toasty; layer beef and onions, cheese, lettuce, and sliced tomatoes on bottom half of bun. Add top half of bun, press together lightly, and eat at once.

Wisconsin

Milwaukee is known as the beer capital of the world. Americans drink an average of six gallons of beer per person per year. However, in this beer drinking city each citizen consumes forty-two gallons a year on average.

Milwaukee Beer Beef Party Stew

Milwaukee is a city that really enjoys beer and sports. It is home to many of America's most famous breweries, so it is only natural that its citizens enjoy using beer in their cooking. This stew can easily be made a day ahead for a party and will taste all the better, as the flavors will have a chance to mellow.

- 3 POUNDS CHUCK, ROUND, OR STEWING BEEF CUT IN 1½-INCH CUBES
- ¾ CUP FLOUR (FOR DREDGING)
- 4 TABLESPOONS OIL OR BACON FAT
- 5 LARGE ONIONS (ANY VARIETY), PEELED AND SLICED
- 3 CUPS BEER
- 1 10½-OUNCE CAN BEEF BOUILLON
- 3 GARLIC CLOVES, PEELED AND MINCED
- 1 TABLESPOON MINCED PARSLEY
- PINCH OF THYME
- 1 BAY LEAF
- SALT AND PEPPER TO TASTE
- 1 TABLESPOON BROWN SUGAR
- 1 TABLESPOON WINE VINEGAR

Pat the meat dry with paper towels and dredge in flour. Heat the oil or bacon fat in a heavy stew pot and brown the beef in batches. When finished, set the beef aside, put the onions in the pot, and lightly brown, adding more oil if needed. Return beef to the pot. Add beer, bouillon, garlic, herbs, salt, and pepper. Stir well. Cover pot and bake in a 325° oven for 2½ hours or until meat is tender. During the last 10 minutes of cooking, stir in the sugar and vinegar. It may be necessary to add additional beer during cooking if the liquid is not covering the beef. Serve the stew to 6 with boiled potatoes and mugs of cold beer.

Red Flannel Hash for a Winter Evening

Vermont

In colonial times, New England ladies had to be practical and thrifty with their cooking time. "New England boiled dinner" leftovers could easily be turned into the next day's "red flannel hash," so called because the beets give a fresh reddish glow to the hash. This modern version is easy and most satisfying.

- 4 MEDIUM POTATOES, COOKED, PEELED, AND CHOPPED (ABOUT 3 CUPS)
- 6 MEDIUM BEETS, COOKED, PEELED, AND CHOPPED (ABOUT 1½ CUPS)
- 1½ CUPS COOKED CORNED BEEF BRISKET, CUT IN SMALL PIECES
- 3 GREEN ONIONS, MINCED
- SALT AND PEPPER TO TASTE
- ¼ CUP LIQUID: RED WINE, STOCK, OR MILK
- ¼ CUP BACON DRIPPINGS, BUTTER, OIL, OR A COMBINATION OF THESE
- 3–6 EGGS: 1 OR 2 PER PERSON (OPTIONAL)
- PARSLEY (FOR GARNISH)
- RED PEPPER SAUCE (OPTIONAL)

Combine all ingredients except the last 4 in a bowl and mix thoroughly. Heat the drippings in a frying pan until hot. Place the hash in the pan and pat down with a spatula. Cook over medium flame for 15 minutes and turn over, moving so that the crispy parts mingle with the hash. Then cook for another 15 minutes. At this point, eggs (if desired) may be broken (like fried eggs) over the hash; cover and cook until the eggs are firm. Garnish with parsley and dapple a few drops of hot sauce on top if you want. Serve to 3 on warmed plates.

In the mountains of Vermont, this was a popular dish with Ethan Allen and his Green Mountain Boys.

California

This makes a good party main dish because it can easily be prepared ahead (for a party host or hostess, it is always advisable to avoid last-minute rushing around the kitchen!).

Los Angeles Classic Tamale Pie

Tamale pie is a unique combination of Californian and Mexican flavors. This casserole has been a favorite of American cooks for many decades.

Cornmeal Crust

- 5 CUPS WATER
- 2½ CUPS CORNMEAL
- 1 TEASPOON SALT
- 1 TEASPOON CHILI POWDER
- 1 TABLESPOON BUTTER OR OLIVE OIL

To make the crust, bring water to boil in a large pot, and then reduce heat to simmer. Slowly pour in the cornmeal, seasonings, and butter or oil. Stir with a wooden spoon to blend. Continue cooking over a low flame for 15 minutes, stirring now and then to prevent mixture from sticking to the bottom. Set aside.

Filling

- 1 TABLESPOON VEGETABLE OIL OR BACON DRIPPINGS
- 1 POUND GROUND BEEF
- 1 TABLESPOON CHILI POWDER
- 1 TEASPOON CUMIN (OPTIONAL)
- SALT TO TASTE

1 MEDIUM ONION, PEELED AND CHOPPED
1 MEDIUM GREEN OR RED BELL PEPPER, CHOPPED
1 28-OUNCE CAN DICED OR SOLID-PACK TOMATOES, UNDRAINED (OR 2 CUPS FRESH, CHOPPED)
1 CUP FRESH CORN (SCRAPED FROM COB) OR 1 CUP DRAINED CANNED OR FROZEN CORN
ANAHEIM OR DICED GREEN CHILES (OPTIONAL)

To make the filling, heat the oil in a large frying pan. Then add meat and seasonings. Stir around to blend. Add onion and green pepper. Fry until meat loses pink color. Now add tomatoes and corn. If using frozen corn, cook as per package instructions and then add. Some cooks like to add additional Anaheim chiles or diced green chiles, but this is up to your taste. Simmer for 20 minutes, stirring now and then. Remove from heat.

Topping

1 CUP GRATED CHEDDAR CHEESE
1 CUP PITTED, SLICED BLACK OLIVES

To Assemble

Lightly grease a 2-quart shallow baking dish or casserole dish. Line with ⅔ of the cornmeal mixture. Add filling, and top with remaining crust. You may have to dip your hands in cold water and sort of pat this top crust around. Sprinkle with grated cheese and olives. Bake at 350° for 40 minutes. This will serve 6–8, depending on appetites.

Tamale pie is traditionally served with hot tortillas and a green salad. Cold beer is the perfect beverage for this Los Angeles supper.

West Virginia

Harper's Ferry Pulled Pork Sandwiches

Pulled pork sandwiches are the all-around darlings of the South's sandwich world. One of the best I ever tasted was in the historic city of Harper's Ferry, where the little hillside cafes that line the meandering road to the river offer cool beer with these tasty sandwiches. The secret is a fresh and sturdy bun filled with just the right amount of that smoky, tender pork. This can be a great summer party dish.

Pulled pork is simply a piece of pork cooked so long (either in the oven or barbecued) that it is tender enough to be pulled into shreds.

- 1 PORK SHOULDER ROAST (5–6 POUNDS)
- ⅓ CUP WRIGHT'S OR OTHER LIQUID SMOKE
- SALT AND PEPPER (FOR ROAST)
- 2 GARLIC CLOVES, MINCED
- SALT AND PEPPER TO TASTE (FOR SAUCE)
- PAN JUICES
- 4 CUPS KETCHUP
- 2 TABLESPOONS TABASCO OR OTHER HOT SAUCE
- HAMBURGER BUNS OR OTHER STYLE ROLLS FOR THE SANDWICHES

The meat can be barbecued in a smoker until well done and then cooled and shredded. A quicker, easier method is to score (make cuts in) the meat on both sides to a ½-inch depth and rub with liquid smoke, salt, and pepper. Wrap with double foil and bake for 4 hours in a 325° oven, on a rack set in a baking pan. Cool and shred. Mix remaining ingredients (except buns) together with pork. This may be done ahead and the mixture warmed before serving, in a casserole dish in the oven. Set the dish on the table and serve buffet-style with a basket of buns. This should feed a party of 20.

Missouri Swiss Steak

Missouri

My mother made Swiss steak, and my mother-in-law made it too. Swiss steak is in almost every American cookbook and is certainly a Midwest favorite. It is easy and hearty. I like mine with mashed potatoes, but some prefer noodles.

- 2 POUNDS ROUND STEAK, ABOUT ½ INCH THICK
- ½ CUP FLOUR
- SALT AND PEPPER TO TASTE
- 3 TABLESPOONS VEGETABLE OR CANOLA OIL
- 3 TABLESPOONS BUTTER
- 1 LARGE ONION, SLICED THINLY (ABOUT 1 CUP)
- 2 CLOVES GARLIC, MINCED
- 2 CUPS WATER
- 1 14-OUNCE CAN DICED OR WHOLE TOMATOES, UNDRAINED
- 2 CARROTS, CUT IN HALF
- ½ CUP RED OR WHITE WINE (OPTIONAL)
- MINCED PARSLEY (FOR GARNISH)

Cut the steak into serving-size pieces. Mix the flour with salt and pepper in a flat pan. Dredge each piece of the steak, rubbing in the flour. Heat the oil and butter in a large frying pan. Fry each piece of steak until brown on each side, adding additional butter and oil as needed. Remove to a large baking casserole dish. When all the meat is browned, add the sliced onion and garlic to pan and stir-fry until limp. Add to the meat. Place 2 cups of water in the frying pan and stir to gather up juices left in pan. Add to meat along with tomatoes, carrots, and wine if used. Add additional water or stock if liquid does not cover the meat. Cover and bake at 350° for 1½ hours or until meat is tender. (This step may also be done on top of the stove, but I think the oven gives a better flavor.) To serve, garnish with parsley and serve with mashed potatoes (or noodles) to 4.

This is one of those dishes that is improved by preparing a day ahead.

Washington, D.C.

Creamy chicken hash was a favorite of President Andrew Jackson. Household journals show that his cook added a dash of white wine to the family's breakfast chicken hash for extra piquant flavor. A visit to the Hermitage, the Jackson family home near Nashville, Tennessee, is an American historic experience not to be missed.

POULTRY

Capitol Creamy Chicken Hash

Power breakfasts in Washington, D.C., are an important part of the political process. Over these breakfasts, vital political decisions are discussed informally, friendships are made, and tidbits about the social world of the city are exchanged. Chicken hash has always been popular for this morning meal.

- 3–4 CUPS FINELY CUBED COOKED CHICKEN
- 1 CUP FRESH CHOPPED MUSHROOMS (OPTIONAL)
- 1 GREEN ONION, DICED
- 1 CUP CREAM (OR LEFTOVER CHICKEN GRAVY: CHICKEN JUICES PLUS FLOUR)
- 2 TABLESPOONS FRESH MINCED PARSLEY
- SALT AND PEPPER TO TASTE
- PINCH OF NUTMEG
- 2 TABLESPOONS BUTTER
- 2 TABLESPOONS VEGETABLE OIL OR BACON DRIPPINGS

Place ingredients through nutmeg in a bowl and mix together. Melt butter and oil in a 12-inch frying pan until hot, but not bubbling. Add the hash mixture. Cook 4 minutes over medium-high heat. Reduce heat, cover pan, and cook an additional 10 minutes (don't stir). Flop out of the pan onto a warmed platter so the browned side is facing up. This will serve 4 and goes splendidly with bacon and poached eggs!

Greenwich Village Chicken Cacciatore

Years ago, when Gordon and I moved from California to New York, I wanted to live in Greenwich Village. It sounded very bohemian and seemed the perfect spot for my art-student husband and me. Unfortunately, it had been taken over by wealthy people, and the rents were not affordable on our GI allowance, so we ended up living in half an apartment in Astoria. However, we could afford to dine in the village in the Italian family restaurants. On a recent visit, it was a joy to find that hearty Italian fare could still be found at moderate prices in colorful Greenwich Village.

- 1 3–4 POUND CHICKEN, CUT UP (OR 3–4 POUNDS OF CHICKEN PARTS)
- ½ CUP FLOUR
- ¼ CUP OLIVE OIL
- 1 MEDIUM ONION, CHOPPED
- 2 CLOVES FRESH GARLIC, MINCED
- ¼ CUP RED OR WHITE WINE VINEGAR
- ½ TEASPOON DRIED OR FRESH OREGANO
- ½ TEASPOON DRIED FRESH THYME
- SALT AND PEPPER TO TASTE
- 2 CUPS CANNED WHOLE TOMATOES
- 1 RED OR GREEN BELL PEPPER, CHOPPED
- 1 CUP SLICED FRESH MUSHROOMS
- ¼ CUP CHOPPED BLACK OLIVES
- ¼ CUP WHITE WINE

New York

Italian immigrants arriving at Ellis Island carried salami, cheese, wine, olive oil, grape cuttings from home vineyards, and treasured family recipes. They had a major influence on the culinary menu of New York. Today, this spirited type of cuisine remains the most popular in the city.

Coat the chicken with flour. The simplest way to do this is by the old-fashioned method of placing the flour in a paper bag, adding the chicken, and then shaking to coat with flour.

Heat oil in a large frying pan. Brown (fry) chicken on both sides (this may have to be done in 2 batches). Remove the chicken and add onion and garlic to the pan. Fry just until limp, and then stir in wine vinegar and seasonings. Add tomatoes, breaking up any large pieces. Next, add pepper, mushrooms, olives, wine, and chicken. Cover and simmer until chicken is tender—about 45 minutes. This dish can also be baked in a 350° oven for 45 minutes. Your favorite pasta may be served with the chicken. Be sure to have some crusty Italian bread to dunk in the flavorful juices. This will serve 4–5.

Louisiana

Myrtle Grove Plantation Gumbo

"Nana" was my grandmother on my mother's side of our family. Because I was her first grandchild, I was special to her; we had a lot in common and were very close. I was the perfect audience for her tales of plantation life at Myrtle Grove. In the early mornings, shrimp sellers would come to the plantation, offering the finest Gulf shrimp. There were chickens in the barnyard, and there was ham in the smokehouse. Okra grew in the plantation gardens. The ingredients were all combined for the delicious plantation gumbo. The Wilkinsons always had large bowls of hot rice to accompany this dish.

Gumbo is a Bantu word for okra; gumbo is usually thickened with okra.

The first years my husband and I were married, we lived in an apartment in Hermosa Beach, California, next to Nana. She had designed this Hermosa Beach apartment with long Southern-style hallways to spend summers away from her hot Pasadena home. When we would come home from school and work, Nana often had gumbo waiting for our dinner. It tasted wonderful, as Nana was a gumbo master.

Years later, when we visited New Orleans, a friend drove us down the Mississippi River road to see if the Myrtle Grove plantation was still standing. Alas, a hurricane had blown it away decades ago. Luckily, I was able to find an old photo of it. Myrtle Grove really did look like my childhood dream fantasy of Tara from *Gone with the Wind.* Gumbo is a perfect party dish, and if made a day ahead, the flavors will mellow beautifully.

- ¼ CUP OIL (TO FRY THE CHICKEN IN)
- 1 CHICKEN (ABOUT 3 POUNDS), CUT UP
- 1 CUP DICED HAM (TASSO, IF AVAILABLE)
- 1 LARGE ONION, CHOPPED
- SALT AND PEPPER TO TASTE
- 2 TABLESPOONS PARSLEY
- 1 28-OUNCE CAN SOLID-PACK TOMATOES, UNDRAINED
- 1 CUP WHITE WINE (OPTIONAL)
- 3 CUPS OKRA (FRESH, FROZEN, OR CANNED)
- 1 POUND MEDIUM SHRIMP, PEELED AND DEVEINED

In a large frying pan, fry the chicken pieces, ham, and onion in the oil until lightly browned. This procedure is a sort of light stir-fry to give a toasty flavor and seal in the chicken juices. Remove to a large soup pot or Dutch oven. Add salt, pepper, parsley, and tomatoes, cutting up any large pieces of tomato. If you wish, 1 cup of white wine can be added for extra zest. The liquid should just cover the chicken; if it seems low, add extra water. Cover and simmer until the chicken is tender, about 50 minutes.

Remove chicken and cool until it is easy to handle. Remove meat from the bones, cutting into bite-sized pieces. Return chicken meat to the pot. Cut okra in ½-inch slices; add okra and shrimp to chicken mixture and cook uncovered over medium heat for about 10 minutes. (My Nana did not use filé powder, as she felt the okra provided enough thickening.) Serve to 6 with generous portions of steamed rice.

Tasso ham is a special Southern smoked ham available in many specialty stores.

North Carolina

Georgia

A romantically Southern pastime is to cook Brunswick stew over a hickory-log fire in the woods on a moonlit night.

See photo on pp. 30–31.

Brunswick Stew

Brunswick stew is the subject of intense rivalry in a real Southern stew war. Brunswick County, North Carolina, has issued a proprietary claim. The coastal city of Brunswick, Georgia, claims the stew belongs to it; and then there is Brunswick County, Georgia, which also claims the stew originated there. These stew wars are carried on in the joyous form of Brunswick stew festivals. The tasty mixture is prepared in huge cauldrons (one of them a twenty-five-gallon cast-iron pot) and is stirred with giant wooden paddles.

What is Brunswick stew? One of the legends suggests that it originated when a camp cook for Dr. Creed Haskins's Virginia hunting party prepared a blend of local squirrel, bacon, onions, and stale bread for the hungry returning hunters. Today, chicken has, for the most part, replaced squirrel, and different cooks have their own special recipes.

Dr. Haskins discovered, when he became a member of the House of Delegates, that Brunswick stew added a special conviviality to political gatherings with friends. The stew continues to be served at fund-raisers in the South. This dish is perfect for large parties and may be served with cornbread and coleslaw.

3 POUNDS CHICKEN (PARTS OR WHOLE CHICKEN)
2 QUARTS WATER (2 CUPS MAY BE WHITE WINE)
2 MEDIUM ONIONS, CHOPPED
2 CUPS DICED TOMATOES (CANNED OR FRESH)
SALT AND PEPPER TO TASTE
3 MEDIUM POTATOES, PEELED AND CHOPPED (1½–2 CUPS)
1 10-OUNCE PACKAGE FROZEN LIMA BEANS (DO NOT THAW)
2 CUPS FRESH, FROZEN, OR CANNED CORN

Place chicken in a stew pot. Cover with water; add onions, tomatoes, salt, and pepper. Cover and simmer until tender, about 1 hour. Remove chicken from broth, cool, and remove meat. Cut into small bite-sized pieces. While you are preparing the chicken, simmer the potatoes (covered) in the broth for about 20 minutes. When potatoes are tender, add the chicken, lima beans, and corn and continue to simmer covered for another 30 minutes. Serve to 6 in soup bowls. Like all stews, this one tastes even better the next day.

Thanksgiving Roast Turkey with Mushroom Sage Dressing

Iowa

Thanksgiving is a national holiday that unites all Americans in a most special way. It is a day when family and friends sit together and reflect on the many things we as Americans can be thankful for. The center of this celebration is traditionally a turkey feast.

In our nation's heartland, with its endless, beautiful, rich farmlands, Thanksgiving dinner is the height of American tradition. Mushrooms have long been hunted in this region's forests and are popular in Thanksgiving turkey dressings.

Benjamin Franklin wanted the turkey to be our national emblem instead of the eagle. Certainly, turkey is dearer to our stomachs!

Mushroom Sage Dressing

- ½ cup butter
- ¾ cup chopped onion (1 large)
- 1 medium loaf good-quality day-old white bread, torn into small pieces (to make about 8–9 cups)
- 1½ cups chopped celery with leaves
- 3 tablespoons fresh minced parsley
- 2 tablespoons fresh or dried sage
- Salt and pepper to taste
- 1 pound fresh mushrooms (brown if available), sliced

The turkey is native to North and Central America. A male is called a tom, and a female, a hen.

Turkey Stock and Gravy

- NECK AND GIBLETS (HEART, LIVER, AND GIZZARD) FROM YOUR FRESH TURKEY
- 6 CUPS WATER
- ¾ CUP CHOPPED ONION (1 LARGE)
- 1 CUP CHOPPED CELERY
- SALT AND PEPPER TO TASTE (FOR STOCK)
- 1 BAY LEAF
- SALT AND PEPPER TO TASTE (FOR GRAVY)
- 3 TABLESPOONS FLOUR (FOR GRAVY)

Roast Turkey

- 1 FRESH TURKEY (12–15 POUNDS)
- SALT, PEPPER, AND PAPRIKA
- ¼ CUP BUTTER, MELTED

To prepare the dressing, melt the ½ cup butter in a large (preferably iron) frying pan. Add ¾ cup onion and cook over medium heat, stirring, just until limp. Add bread crumbs, celery, parsley, sage, salt, pepper, and mushrooms. Cook over medium heat and stir-fry for about 10 minutes; the bread should be lightly browned. Remove from pan, place in a bowl, and refrigerate. To leave more time for fun on Thanksgiving, it is best to make the dressing the evening before (but do NOT put it into the turkey at this time!). If you like a moister dressing, just before stuffing the turkey add 1 cup stock or white wine and gently mix with bread mixture.

To prepare stock for gravy and dressing, place the turkey neck and giblets in a pan with 6 cups water, 1 chopped onion, 1 cup chopped celery, salt and pepper, and a bay leaf. Cover and simmer for 1 hour, and then set aside.

To roast the turkey, pat the cavity dry using paper towels. Sprinkle with salt and pepper. Spoon the dressing loosely in the cavity and stitch or skewer to close turkey skin. Dressing expands while cooking, so if you have any left over, simply bake it in a well-oiled pan for 30 minutes at 350°. Place the turkey on a flat rack in a large, flat roasting pan, breast side up. Sprinkle skin with salt, pepper, and paprika. Bake turkey 15–20 minutes for each pound. Baste turkey with melted butter about every 30 minutes. When cooked, the internal temperature on a meat thermometer (inserted into the meatiest part of the breast) should be 180° F. Do not overcook. Let the turkey rest on a warmed platter while you make the gravy.

To make gravy, remove the giblets from your stock. Pour off fat from turkey pan, leaving 3 tablespoons. Slowly add 3 tablespoons flour to the fat and blend until smooth over medium heat. To the fat/flour mixture, slowly add (while stirring) 3 cups of your stock and salt and pepper to taste. Stir until smooth. This will take about 6 minutes. Chop the giblets and add to the gravy.

To serve: Garnish turkey platter with watercress or parsley. Remove stuffing from turkey and place in a warmed bowl. Slice turkey. A 12-pound turkey will serve about 9 with leftovers.

Serve with traditional Thanksgiving foods, such as mashed potatoes, yams, creamed onions, cranberry sauce, pumpkin pie, or whatever dishes are traditional in your family. For some, the best part of Thanksgiving is turkey sandwiches the next day.

Virginia

President Thomas Jefferson was celebrated for his White House entertaining. State dinners began at four in the afternoon. Guests sat at one round table, which President Jefferson preferred for amicable conversation. Seating was first come, first served. During his two terms in office, Jefferson spent more than $10,000 just for wine. This was paid for by the president's private income.

SEAFOOD

Thomas Jefferson Deviled Crab

This renaissance president was a native of Virginia and had a special fondness for such Southern foods as deviled crab. Jefferson loved wine and entertaining. At the end of his first year in the White House, his entertainment expenses exceeded $12,000—more than the presidential income. Of course, because he was an impeccable president, it was paid for out of his personal funds.

If you do not live near a good source for fresh crab, frozen may be substituted in this recipe. A glass of cool dry white wine adds a nice touch when served with this delicious dish.

- ¼ CUP BUTTER
- 1 MEDIUM RED PEPPER, CHOPPED
- 4 GREEN ONIONS, MINCED
- 1 TABLESPOON FLOUR
- 2 CUPS HALF-AND-HALF
- ¼ TEASPOON CAYENNE
- 1 TABLESPOON DIJON-STYLE MUSTARD
- 2 TABLESPOONS BRANDY OR WHITE WINE
- 1 POUND FRESH CRABMEAT (IMITATION CRAB MAY BE USED)
- BUTTER (FOR DISH)
- ¼ CUP BREAD CRUMBS
- MINCED PARSLEY (FOR GARNISH)

Melt the butter in a heavy saucepan. Add the pepper and onion. Fry over a low flame just until limp. Add the flour to the pan and blend well. Next, add the half-and-half, cayenne, and mustard. Stir over low flame until the mixture is slightly thick. Add liquor and crabmeat.

Place in a 2–3 quart buttered baking dish or 4 individual dishes or baking shells. Sprinkle the bread crumbs on top and bake at 350° for 20 minutes. Garnish with minced parsley. This will serve 4.

Delilah's Utah Clam Casserole

Utah

My mother-in-law, Maureen, was born in the small town of Payson in northern Utah. She came to Long Beach, California, as a bride but always returned to her hometown for a part of every year to visit with her large family. In later years, Maureen was able to move back permanently to this place she loved. When at age eighty-four she passed away, there was a large church service and graveyard burial. At the end of the ceremonies, all the family and many friends returned to her home. We arrived to find gifts of ready-to-eat food from family and friends filling the table. Everyone was able to share in the feast and memories of a special lady. One of my favorites was this tasty casserole from her friend Delilah.

GREASE (FOR BAKING DISH)
2 CUPS UNCOOKED POTATOES, CUT IN STRIPS (ABOUT 2½" X ½")
1 CUP CARROTS, CUT IN STRIPS
1 6½-OUNCE CAN CHOPPED CLAMS, UNDRAINED
1 MEDIUM ONION, PEELED AND SLICED
1 STICK (4 OUNCES) BUTTER
SALT AND PEPPER TO TASTE
½ TEASPOON DILL SEED OR WEED

Lightly grease a 2-quart baking casserole dish. Place the potato strips in the bottom. Next layer the carrots, followed by clams with juice, and finally the onion. Melt the butter with seasonings and pour over casserole. Bake at 350° covered, for 45 minutes.

After baking, you can sprinkle this dish with paprika and fresh parsley, if desired.

Hawaii

Baked Opakapaka in Orange Citrus Sauce

Opakapaka, a fish of the snapper family, is abundant in Hawaiian waters and is one of the most popular entrées at Hawaiian diners. On the mainland, where opakapaka is hard to come by, you can make this dish with red snapper. Baking fish is an easy and healthy way to prepare it. Hot steamed rice and chilled cucumber slices are the perfect accompaniment for this dish.

- ¼ CUP FRESH ORANGE JUICE
- 1 TEASPOON GRATED ORANGE RIND
- 1 TABLESPOON SOY SAUCE
- 1 TABLESPOON SESAME OIL
- 2 TABLESPOONS MINCED GREEN ONION TOPS
- SALT AND PEPPER TO TASTE
- 1 POUND OPAKAPAKA (OR RED SNAPPER) BONELESS FILLETS
- ORANGE SLICES FOR GARNISH (OPTIONAL)

Combine all the ingredients except fish and orange slices in a shallow baking dish large enough to accommodate all the fish in a single layer. Stir with a fork to bland. Add fish and cover with marinade. Place in refrigerator to marinate for 1 hour.

Heat oven to 400°. Place the pan in the oven, uncovered, and bake 10–15 minutes or until fish is done. Baste fish with sauce once during baking. Be careful not to overcook. To serve, place the fish with sauce on 2 warmed plates. You may want to add a few thin orange slices for garnish. This will serve 2.

This dish is also delicious served cold for hot-weather dining.

San Antonio River Walk Shrimp Enchiladas

Of the many American "restaurant rows," the River Walk in the historic city of San Antonio is certainly one of the most unique. Lush tropical plants line the 2½-mile walk. Sightseeing boats wind up and down the gentle river. It is sort of an American version of Venice. But the River Walk almost never even came into being. After years of devastating floods, the city had decided to pave over the river and turn it into an underground sewer. But a group of devoted Texas ladies had a vision that this area could be turned into a beautiful relaxing recreational space and those ladies waged a vigorous campaign to save the *Paseo del Rio*. Under President Franklin D. Roosevelt, the WPA was enlisted for the construction of bridges and paths. The women's vision and steadfastness paid off, and today this walk is famous around the world. The restaurants that line the path are inviting; one can stroll and view menus and diners before selecting a dining spot. Many feature a special style of Tex-Mex cuisine with a Spanish influence. These menus offer many versions of enchiladas. I especially enjoyed this version, prepared with fresh Gulf shrimp.

Texas

You may buy cooked shrimp or cook your own by simmering fresh shrimp in 1 quart of salted boiling water, uncovered, until shrimp turn pink—about 8 minutes.

In San Antonio, Texas, enchiladas are typically served with refried or black beans and rice.

Enchiladas

- Juice of 1 fresh lime (about 2 tablespoons)
- ½ teaspoon liquid smoke
- 1 pound cooked medium shrimp (see sidebar, p. 57), peeled, deveined, and tails removed
- Salt and pepper to taste
- 1 cup grated Monterey Jack cheese
- 1 cup sour cream
- 2 green onions, minced
- 2 tablespoons diced fresh or canned green chiles
- 6 large flour tortillas
- Grease (for baking dish)

Topping

- 1 cup sour cream
- 1 cup Monterey Jack cheese
- Fresh cilantro for top garnish (about 2 tablespoons snipped in small pieces)

In a stainless steel or glass bowl, combine the lime and liquid smoke. Place shrimp in the bowl. Add salt and pepper. Stir around so shrimp are covered with flavorings. Refrigerate to marinate at least 1 hour, up to 12 hours.

In a larger bowl, combine 1 cup cheese with 1 cup sour cream, green onions, and chiles. Add shrimp with flavorings. Do not drain. This is your filling. To fill flour tortillas, warm each tortilla in a heated iron frying pan until pliable. Divide filling into 6 portions. Place 1 portion of filling in center of each heated tortilla and roll up. It will look like a tube. Place seam side down in a lightly greased baking dish. Combine topping ingredients (except cilantro) and spoon over top. Bake at 350° for 25 minutes. Sprinkle with cilantro. This will make 3 servings.

Idaho

Trout was quite a favorite of Franz Schubert, who composed a song and quartet "Die Forelle," about this lovely, shimmering water creature.

Idaho Rainbow Trout

Travel posters from Idaho always include a picture of a fisherman standing in a woodsy scenic setting, casting his fishing line in a rippling stream. It is true that scenes like this can be found everywhere in Idaho. Many fishermen, including Ernest Hemingway, have visited this state to lure away the trout from rivers and streams.

If you have tasted freshly caught trout fried over a campfire, you know this is the very best; but the next best is trout from your local supermarket. Trout is a plentiful fish available in most markets all year, shipped fresh or frozen.

- 4 FRESH OR FROZEN TROUT (ABOUT 8 OUNCES EACH), CLEANED
- FLOUR (FOR DUSTING)
- SALT AND PEPPER TO TASTE (FOR TROUT)
- ¼ CUP COOKING OIL
- ½ CUP BUTTER
- ½ POUND FRESH MUSHROOMS, SLICED
- SALT AND PEPPER TO TASTE (FOR MUSHROOMS)
- LEMON WEDGES AND PARSLEY (FOR GARNISH)

If using frozen trout, thaw. Pat the trout dry. Dust with flour. Sprinkle with salt and pepper. Heat oil and half the butter (¼ cup) in a large, preferably iron, frying pan. When well heated, add the trout. Brown well on both sides, about 5 minutes on each side. Meanwhile, in another frying pan, melt the remaining ¼ cup butter over a medium flame. Gently fry the mushrooms with a sprinkling of salt and pepper just until light brown. Remove from heat.

When the trout is done, place on a warm serving platter and top with mushrooms. Garnish with the lemon and parsley. Traditionally, this is served with plain boiled potatoes. This will serve 4.

EGGS

Kentucky Scramble for a Brunch

Leisurely breakfasts are a way of life in Kentucky. This splendid combination of corn and peppers folded in with scrambled eggs is delightful to look at and even better to feast upon. It goes well with potatoes and fresh cornbread.

- 8 LEAN SLICES BACON
- 1 CUP CORN KERNELS, PREFERABLY FRESH (CAN ALSO BE CANNED OR FROZEN)
- 1 MEDIUM GREEN PEPPER, FINELY CHOPPED
- ¼ CUP FINELY CHOPPED PIMIENTO OR RED PEPPER
- 3 GREEN ONION TOPS, FINELY SLICED
- 10 EGGS
- SALT AND PEPPER TO TASTE
- ½ TEASPOON TABASCO OR OTHER RED PEPPER SAUCE (OPTIONAL)

Cook bacon in a large skillet until crisp. Remove and place on paper towels to absorb fat. Add the vegetables to the drippings remaining in the pan and cook uncovered over medium heat until wilted, about 5 minutes. With a whisk, beat the eggs together with salt and pepper (and hot sauce, if used). Add to vegetable mixture. Stir over low heat until eggs are set but still creamy. Divide into 6 portions on warmed plates. Crumble the bacon and garnish each portion with the bacon crumbles. This will serve 6.

Kentucky

Mint juleps are the favored drink for breakfast or any time of a Kentucky day. *See recipe on p. 4.*

Desserts

Mississippi

You can use day-old bread for this recipe, if desired.

Delta Queen Bread Pudding

To drift down the Mississippi on the Delta Queen steamboat is an incomparable adventure. The Queen is the smallest of the Delta fleet, and because of this the trip seems like a leisurely cruise with intimate friends. The ship pulls up to the riverbanks (a rope is just latched around a tree) of historic American towns, where fascinating shore trips are offered.

Delicious food is served in the Queen's vintage dining room. There are samples of Southern food every day: collard greens, grits, gumbo, jambalaya, and sumptuous desserts, including this bread pudding, which is one of my favorites. The sous-chef, Mr. Huff, shared his recipe for it, which is presented here in a smaller-sized version for home use.

- 1 LARGE LOAF GOOD-QUALITY WHITE BREAD
- 1 CUP PECAN PIECES
- ¾ CUP RAISINS
- 3 EGGS
- 2½ CUPS MILK
- 1½ CUPS SUGAR
- 1 TABLESPOON CINNAMON
- 3 TABLESPOONS VANILLA
- ⅛ CUP BUTTER, MELTED
- BUTTER (FOR PAN)

Cut bread into 2-inch cubes to make about 5 cups and place in a large mixing bowl. Add pecans and raisins. In a separate bowl, mix eggs, milk, sugar, cinnamon, vanilla, and melted butter together until well blended. Pour over the bread and allow it to soak up the mixture (about 30 minutes). Pour into a well-buttered 2-quart baking pan. Bake at 350° for 40–45 minutes until golden brown and the center springs up when pushed down. Serve warm with whiskey sauce. This will make 6 servings.

Whiskey Sauce

- 1 CUP BUTTER
- 1 CUP BROWN SUGAR
- 3 TABLESPOONS WHISKEY

Melt butter, blend in sugar, and cook together over a medium flame 3 minutes. Add whiskey and cook an additional minute. Serve hot on top of pudding.

The golden age of riverboat travel was from 1870 to 1900. During this period, as many as 12,000 steamboats floated down American rivers. On these floating palaces, guests were treated to elegant dining. The larger boats spent about $2,000 a week on food. This was at a period when chickens sold for ten cents and butter cost five cents a pound.

Oregon

Rogue Valley Poached Pears

Oregon's Rogue River winds along for 215 miles before it finally meets the Pacific Ocean. This scenic river is popular for fishing, and Clark Gable and Zane Grey were both big fans of the Rogue. The valleys alongside the river, especially those near Medford, are famed for their pear orchards. One of the best local ways of preparing pears is this simple poaching. This dessert is refreshing and most attractive.

See photo on pp. 62–63.

- 4 ripe pears (Bartlett, Anjou, Comice, etc.)
- 1 lemon, juice and grated rind
- 1 cup sugar
- ½ teaspoon cinnamon
- 1 teaspoon vanilla
- 3 cups water
- For garnish: honey and toasted hazelnuts, berries simmered in sugar

Peel pears, leaving stems on. In a saucepan, combine lemon juice, lemon rind, sugar, cinnamon, and vanilla with water. Add pears, stir, and bring to a simmer. Cook over a low flame for 8–10 minutes. The pears should be just barely tender, not mushy. You may need to roll them around during the cooking so all of each pear is covered. Cool in the syrup. To serve, remove from syrup and place with stems up on plates. Drizzle honey over each pear and sprinkle with a few toasted, slivered hazelnuts. Sometimes, in Oregon, the pears are topped with berries that have been simmered with a little sugar for 3 minutes. This will serve 4.

Maine "Slump & Grunt"

This quaint and unique name is derived from the behavior of men in Maine (and perhaps other states) who consume this dish as a finish to lunch or dinner and then just want to "slump and grunt" and not return to work. In Maine, a rocking chair on the porch is a favorite place for this slumping and grunting. There are several variations of this recipe, but this oven method seems the best.

BUTTER (FOR PAN)
12 OUNCES (ABOUT 1¼ CUPS) FRESH BLUEBERRIES
⅔ CUP SUGAR
¼ TEASPOON NUTMEG
1 CUP FLOUR
2 TEASPOONS BAKING POWDER
¼ TEASPOON SALT
1 TABLESPOON SUGAR
¼ CUP SHORTENING
⅓ CUP MILK
FLOUR (FOR BOARD)
WHIPPING CREAM FOR TOPPING (OPTIONAL)

Lightly butter an 8″ × 8″ baking dish. Mix the blueberries with ⅔ cup sugar and nutmeg. Place in the baking dish. In a bowl, mix the flour, baking powder, salt, and 1 tablespoon sugar. Work in the shortening with a pastry blender or fork, and then blend in the milk.

Toss dough on a floured board. Pat together and then roll dough about ¼ inch thick. Cut in circles or any desired shape and place on top of the blueberries. Bake at 400° until top is brown, about 20 minutes. This is best served warm. In Maine, thick cream (may be whipped) is served on top. This will serve 6.

Maine

Native Americans called blueberries "star berries." This was because the berry tip forms a perfect five-pointed star.

Massachusetts

Chocolate chip cookies were certainly not part of the Pilgrims' dessert diet. In fact, these cookies did not arrive on the American culinary scene until FDR was in the White House.

These cookies freeze very well.

Massachusetts Toll House Chocolate Chip Cookies

In the late 1930s, Ruth Wakefield, the owner of the Whitman, Massachusetts, Toll House Inn (on the road from Boston to New Bedford), added chopped chocolate to her cookie dough while experimenting with an antiquated recipe from Amelia Simmons. They were such a big hit that eventually a special machine was developed to mold the chocolate into "chips." The cookies' name and recipe were sold to the Nestlé Chocolate Company, which prints the original recipe on every bag of chocolate chips. This recipe is a popular variation of the original.

- ¾ CUP BUTTER
- ¾ CUP WHITE SUGAR
- ¾ CUP BROWN SUGAR
- 2 EGGS
- 3 TABLESPOONS MILK
- 1 TEASPOON VANILLA
- 2¼ CUPS FLOUR
- 1 TEASPOON BAKING SODA
- ¼ TEASPOON SALT
- 1 12-OUNCE PACKAGE SEMISWEET CHOCOLATE CHIPS
- 1 CUP CHOPPED WALNUTS OR PECANS
- GREASE (FOR BAKING SHEETS)

In a mixing bowl, cream together the butter and sugars. Add the eggs, milk, and vanilla. Separately, sift dry ingredients together. Add to the bowl, and blend well. Stir in the chips and nuts. Drop dough by tablespoonfuls on lightly greased baking sheets. Bake at 375° for 10–12 minutes. Cookie edges should be brown. Remove from sheets, place on a cookie rack, and cool. Store in airtight containers. This recipe makes about 5 dozen cookies.

Teddy Roosevelt's Christmas Sand Tarts

New York

Theodore Roosevelt loved to entertain guests in his Sagamore Hill home on Christmas morning. This Long Island Victorian residence is now operated by the National Park Service and is open year-round. The grounds are spacious, and the house is filled with mementos. In the kitchen is the large iron stove in which these sand tarts were freshly baked on Christmas mornings.

- ½ CUP BUTTER
- 1 CUP SUGAR
- 2 EGGS
- 1 TEASPOON VANILLA
- 1¾ CUPS FLOUR
- 2 TEASPOONS BAKING POWDER
- ¼ TEASPOON SALT
- GREASE (FOR COOKIE SHEET)
- 4 TABLESPOONS SUGAR MIXED WITH 1 TEASPOON CINNAMON (FOR TOPPING)

Place the butter in a bowl and cream it. Add sugar gradually, mixing until the mixture is light and fluffy. Blend in eggs, one at a time. Blend well and add vanilla. Set aside. Sift the flour with baking powder and salt. Mix with first mixture. Dampen your hands and form a roll with the dough, about 1½ inches in diameter. Wrap in wax paper, and chill at least 2 hours or overnight.

To bake, cut slices (about ¼ inch thick) from the roll and place on a lightly greased cookie sheet. Sprinkle cookie tops with the "sand." Bake at 375° for 10–12 minutes. The cookies should be golden brown. This will make 2 dozen sand tarts.

These cookies, a favorite of Theodore Roosevelt's, are called sand tarts because the sugar and cinnamon sprinkled on top look like sand.

Kansas

Peanut butter was first sold at the St. Louis World's Fair in 1904. It was promoted as a health food by Dr. Ambrose Straub, who created this mixture as a source of protein for his elderly patients who had difficulty chewing.

Wichita Peanut Butter & Jelly Cookies

Americans have a passion for the combination of peanut butter and jelly—from the children who clamor for it in sandwiches for school lunches, to adults who savor a kind of guilty childlike pleasure in the same sandwiches.

While driving across the country on a hot summer day, we stopped at a Wichita cafe. It was blessedly cool inside, and the friendly waitress suggested we taste some of their homemade cookies. With a chilled glass of milk, they made a refreshing interlude in our long drive. When we finally got home to California, I made my own version of this Kansas cookie.

- ½ CUP SHORTENING (CAN BE PART BUTTER)
- ½ CUP PEANUT BUTTER, SMOOTH OR CRUNCHY
- 1 CUP SUGAR
- 1 EGG
- 2 TABLESPOONS MILK
- 1 TEASPOON VANILLA
- ½ TEASPOON BAKING POWDER
- 1¾ CUPS ALL-PURPOSE FLOUR
- ½ CUP JAM, YOUR FAVORITE FLAVOR

Cream shortening, peanut butter, and sugar together. Add egg, milk, and vanilla and blend well. Set aside. Sift baking powder and flour together, add to first mixture, and mix well. Chill in a bowl (for easier handling) for about 15 minutes.

Roll dough into 1-inch balls. Place on an ungreased cookie sheet about 2 inches apart. With your finger, press an indentation in the center of each cookie, and place a small dab of jam in the dent. Do

not overfill, or the jam will run out and burn on the cookie sheet. Bake at 375° for 12–15 minutes, until golden brown. Remove and cool cookies on a rack. This will make about 3½ dozen tasty cookies.

Vermont

This batter may also be poured into well-greased or lined cupcake or muffin tins, in which case baking will take 20–25 minutes.

Vermont Soft Gingerbread—1912

Ginger is used in many ways in New England, and gingerbread is one of the favorites. In some New England states, there used to be a sort of holiday known as Muster Day, when the local men would come to town for militia training. Fortunately, not much time was spent on this drudgery. The highlight of the event was eating gingerbread, sold by vendors and accompanied by rum. This recipe was a favorite of a Vermont great-aunt.

- 2 CUPS FLOUR
- 2 TEASPOONS BAKING POWDER
- ½ TEASPOON BAKING SODA
- ¼ CUP SUGAR
- ½ TEASPOON SALT
- 2 TEASPOONS GINGER
- 1 TEASPOON CINNAMON
- 1 EGG
- ½ CUP MILK
- ½ CUP MOLASSES
- ¼ CUP MELTED BUTTER
- GREASE (FOR PAN)

Sift the dry ingredients together. Set aside in bowl. Beat the egg in another bowl; add milk and molasses. Stir into the flour mixture. Add melted butter and combine well. Pour into a well-greased loaf pan and bake at 350° for 30 minutes.

Cincinnati All-American Brownies

Chocolate brownies are an all-American favorite. They are pleasurably crunched in all our states. Not long ago on a visit to Cincinnati, I heard an inspiring performance by the famed Cincinnati Symphony orchestra. This city's symphony has a tradition of performing a late-morning concert during its music season. Audiences were offered sweets and coffee before the performance. Chocolate brownies placed on silver trays filled tables in the handsome lobby. Of course they were my very first choice.

For even the most novice baker, this recipe is quick and easy to prepare.

- 2 SQUARES (1 OUNCE EACH) UNSWEETENED CHOCOLATE
- ⅓ CUP BUTTER, SHORTENING, OR MIXTURE OF BOTH
- 2 EGGS
- 1 CUP SUGAR (WHITE OR BROWN)
- 1 TEASPOON VANILLA
- ¾ CUP FLOUR
- 1 TEASPOON BAKING POWDER
- ½ TEASPOON SALT
- ¾ CUP CHOPPED WALNUTS
- BUTTER (FOR PAN)

Melt chocolate with butter or shortening in a heavy pan over very low heat. Set aside. In a medium to large bowl, beat the eggs until light, and then add sugar gradually. Next add chocolate mixture and vanilla—this may be done with a mixer or by hand. Sift flour, baking powder, and salt together, mix into egg-chocolate mixture, and blend in walnuts. Place in a buttered 8″ × 8″ or 9″ × 9″ square pan. Bake at 350° for 30–35 minutes. Do not overbake or brownies will be dry. Remove from oven and cool on a rack. While slightly warm, cut into desired size squares.

Indiana

This also may be baked in a 3-quart bundt pan. Be sure to grease and flour well. Cooking in a bundt pan will take a full 35 minutes.

Indiana Devil's Food Coffee Cake

I collect cookbooks and am especially interested in our nation's culinary trends. One cake that has never lost popularity is devil's food. This curious name seems to have something to do with a rather puritanical American thought that devouring rich chocolate food is bad. Angel food cakes are pure white and do not contain anything but light, delicate ingredients, so they are deemed sort of heavenly. Both are long-standing favorites in the American cake menu.

I have friends whose relatives in Indiana regularly attend family reunion picnics. This recipe, from one of those Indiana cousins, is always a favorite at these happy gatherings. The coffee adds to the flavor and texture of the cake.

- 2 CUPS FLOUR
- 1 TEASPOON BAKING POWDER
- 1 TEASPOON BAKING SODA
- 1 TEASPOON SALT
- 1 TEASPOON CINNAMON
- ½ CUP COCOA
- 1½ CUPS SUGAR
- ½ CUP VEGETABLE SHORTENING
- ⅔ CUP BUTTERMILK
- ½ CUP COOLED STRONG COFFEE
- 2 EGGS
- 1 TEASPOON VANILLA
- GREASE AND FLOUR (FOR CAKE PANS)

Sift dry ingredients together in a mixing bowl. Add shortening, ⅓ cup buttermilk, and coffee all at once. Beat for 2 minutes until batter is smooth. Next add remaining ⅓ cup buttermilk, eggs, and vanilla. Beat for 2 minutes. Pour into 2 lightly greased and floured 8-inch layer cake pans and bake at 350° for 30–35 minutes. Cake should bounce back when pressed with finger. Remove from pans and cool on racks. Frost with your favorite cake frosting, or enjoy it plain.

Connecticut

The peak season for rhubarb is May and June. It may be refrigerated for up to 5 days. Rhubarb also freezes well. The leaves are toxic, so use only the stalks.

For basic piecrust recipe, see Washington Apple Pie on p. 80.

Connecticut Strawberry/Rhubarb Pie

In colonial times, pies were a big part of each New England meal. Pies were practical as handy, easy-to-eat food that could be taken on sailing voyages or into the farm fields. The colonists' brick ovens were classified by size as ten-pie ovens or twenty-pie ovens. Housewives would bake many pies at once and then freeze them in the snow or store them in cool cellars.

Rhubarb is known in New England as "pieplant" because it is the first plant to come up in the spring. Strawberries soon follow, so it became popular to combine these two ingredients in a pie. The combined flavors are delicious and refreshing.

- PIE PASTRY FOR A 9-INCH, 2-CRUST PIE (SEE SIDEBAR)
- 2 CUPS WASHED AND HULLED STRAWBERRIES, HALVED
- 2 CUPS RHUBARB, WASHED, CUT INTO 1-INCH PIECES
- 4 TABLESPOONS FLOUR
- 1¼ CUPS SUGAR
- ¼ TEASPOON NUTMEG
- 1 TEASPOON GRATED ORANGE RIND (OPTIONAL)
- 2 TABLESPOONS BUTTER

Combine the strawberries and rhubarb in a bowl. Add flour, sugar, nutmeg, and orange rind (if used) to the bowl and blend together. Place in the bottom piecrust and dot with butter. Carefully put the top crust on and crimp to seal edges. Make deep slits in the top crust so the steam can escape. Bake at 400° for 35–40 minutes, until the crust is golden brown. Serve lukewarm to 6–8.

Lancaster County Shoo-Fly Pie

How did it get this name? Most likely it is because flies were attracted to the sweetness of the molasses. When I tasted this pie in an Amish bakery in Lancaster County, I was surprised at its delicious lightness. Before I knew it, I completely devoured a very large piece of pie and went back for a second.

The pie is layered in the shell, with layers of crumbs alternating with layers of the molasses mixture.

1 UNBAKED 9-INCH PIE SHELL (SEE SIDEBAR)

Crumb Mixture

- 1½ CUPS FLOUR
- ½ CUP SUGAR (CAN BE PART BROWN)
- ½–1 TEASPOON CINNAMON
- ½ TEASPOON BAKING SODA
- ¼ CUP BUTTER, AT ROOM TEMPERATURE

Combine ingredients together in a bowl. My friend Verna, who lived in Pennsylvania for many years, recommended using your hands to rub the mixture together until it is very fine.

Molasses Mixture

- ½ CUP MOLASSES
- ½ CUP HOT OR BOILING WATER
- 1 TEASPOON BAKING SODA
- 1 EGG YOLK

In another bowl, mix the molasses and water; blend in soda and egg yolk. Pour ⅓ of this mixture in the pie shell, and follow with a layer of crumbs. Repeat 2 times. Bake at 375° for 40 minutes.

Pennsylvania

This pie is popular in Pennsylvania as an accompaniment for morning coffee.

For basic piecrust recipe, see Washington Apple Pie on p. 80. For a single crust, use one-half ingredient amounts.

Georgia

For make-ahead convenience, this pie can stay in the freezer for up to a week.

Savannah Ice Cream Pumpkin Pecan Pie

The city of Savannah is a popular destination for many tourists today. This charming and historic Southern city is alluring. It has come a long way since the first settlement of colonists arrived from a debtors' prison in England. The British government hoped these colonists would help protect the newly founded place from the Spaniards and natives. This pie is a Georgia Thanksgiving favorite.

Graham Cracker Crust

½ CUP BUTTER
1½ CUPS GRAHAM CRACKER CRUMBS
3 TABLESPOONS CONFECTIONERS' SUGAR
½ TEASPOON CINNAMON
¼ TEASPOON NUTMEG

Melt the butter. Blend with remaining ingredients. Press into a 9-inch pie pan. Chill 1 hour before filling.

Pie Filling

1 QUART VANILLA ICE CREAM (SLIGHTLY SOFTENED)
½ CUP BROWN SUGAR
1 CUP CANNED PUMPKIN (OR 1 CUP FRESH PUMPKIN, COOKED AND MASHED)
1 TEASPOON CINNAMON
½ TEASPOON NUTMEG
¼ TEASPOON SALT
1 TABLESPOON BRANDY (OPTIONAL)

Topping

1 CUP WHIPPING CREAM

½ CUP TOASTED CHOPPED PECANS

Place the ice cream in a bowl. Add the brown sugar, pumpkin, spices, and brandy (if used). Blend together. Gently place in the pie shell and freeze for at least 6 hours.

To serve: Whip the cream, spread on top of the pie, and sprinkle the pecans over the top. This will serve 6–8.

The word pecan *derives from the Cree word* pagan, *referring to a hard-shelled nut. Because Georgia is the leading producer of pecans in America, it is known as the pecan capital of the United States.*

Washington

It tastes especially fine to have a slice of this pie mid-morning with a cup of hot coffee.

Washington Apple Pie

Although apples grow in nearly every state, Washington leads the nation in their cultivation, and the quality of Washington apples is exceptional. Apple pie is the ultimate American dessert, but it is also a good snack any time of the day. It may be topped with a scoop of vanilla ice cream or a wedge of sharp cheddar cheese.

Basic Crust for a 2-Crust Pie

- 2 CUPS FLOUR
- 1 TEASPOON SALT
- ⅔ CUP SHORTENING OR LARD
- 3 TABLESPOONS (MORE OR LESS) COLD LIQUID (ICE WATER, MILK, OR ORANGE JUICE)
- FLOUR (FOR BOARD)

Place flour and salt in a bowl. Mix in shortening with a fork or pastry mixer until the mixture is broken up into small, pea-sized pieces. Add liquid gradually. When mixture is slightly stiff, form into a ball with your hands. My mother-in-law, Maureen, who taught me how to make a piecrust, always used cold milk as liquid for her excellent piecrusts. Flour a board, and divide dough into 2 balls. Roll 1 out for bottom crust and 1 for top crust. Dough should be rolled out to about ⅛ inch thick. Place bottom crust in a 9-inch pie pan. Set aside top crust until you've filled pie.

Pie Filling

- 1 CUP SUGAR
- 1½ TEASPOONS CORNSTARCH OR 2 TABLESPOONS FLOUR
- 1 TEASPOON CINNAMON
- ½ TEASPOON NUTMEG (OPTIONAL)
- 6–7 CUPS APPLES, PEELED AND CORED, SLICED LENGTHWISE INTO ½-INCH WEDGES
- 1 TABLESPOON LEMON JUICE
- 1–2 TABLESPOONS BUTTER

To prepare filling, mix the sugar, flour or cornstarch, cinnamon, and nutmeg (if used) in a bowl. Add the apple slices and lemon juice. Mix well so slices are evenly coated. Place in piecrust and dot with butter. Gently place top crust over filling. Crimp to seal edges, and make slits in the top crust for steam to escape. Bake at 425° for 60 minutes. Remove from oven and cool on a wire rack. I like to serve the pie slightly warm. This will serve 6.

Pike Place Market opened in Seattle in 1907. It continues to be one of our nation's most treasured markets, with panoramic views and a Northwest atmosphere. At the market, one hundred farmers display their local bounty. In the fall, you can see and taste all the myriad apple varieties of this beautiful area.

California

San Francisco Rum Pie

Rum was one of San Francisco's favorite drinks in the turbulent early days of the city. Rugged miners and sailors used their gold to buy intoxicating beverages, supporting 800 groggeries in the city by 1860. Today, fine wines have largely replaced hard liquors as the preferred social drink, but chocolate pie flavored with rum remains a popular and seductive favorite.

- 1 9-INCH BAKED PIE SHELL (A GRAHAM CRACKER CRUST IS GOOD FOR THIS PIE—SEE SIDEBAR)
- 1 6-OUNCE PACKAGE CHOCOLATE CHIPS
- 3 EGGS (2 SEPARATED)
- 3 TABLESPOONS DARK OR LIGHT RUM
- 1 PINT WHIPPING CREAM
- CHOCOLATE CURLS OR SHAVINGS (FOR GARNISH)

Melt the chocolate chips in a double boiler or heavy pan over low flame. Cool slightly. Add 1 whole egg, plus 2 eggs yolks (reserve whites) and rum. Mix well with mixer at low speed. Beat remaining egg whites in a separate bowl with a mixer until stiff. Fold into the chocolate mixture.

Whip the cream until fairly stiff. Blend 1 cup of the whipped cream into the pie filling, reserving the remaining cup for the topping. Carefully spoon the filling into the pie shell and refrigerate at least 4 hours (overnight is better). To serve, spread the remaining cup of whipped cream over the pie. Garnish with a few chocolate curls or shavings. This will serve 6.

For graham cracker crust recipe, see Key Lime Pie on p. 83.

Key Lime Pie

Early Spanish settlers brought the lime to Florida. The lime trees adapted quickly to the climate of the Florida Keys and have flourished there. These "Key limes" were the same variety that the British Navy used to protect its sailors from scurvy, which earned the sailors the nickname "limeys." They drank the lime juice with rum to make the cure more palatable.

As with any popular American pie, there are many versions of this one. Some are sickly sweet or artificially colored a weird green. My neighbor's sister lives in Florida and offered this excellent recipe, which has the perfect flavor balance.

Florida

An easy way to crush the graham crackers is to put them in a plastic bag and whack them with a rolling pin.

Graham Cracker Crust

- 18 SINGLE GRAHAM CRACKERS
- ¼ CUP MELTED BUTTER
- 2 TABLESPOONS SUGAR
- DASH EACH OF CINNAMON AND NUTMEG

Crush the crackers into fine crumbs. Combine with the butter, sugar, and spices. Mix with your hands or a spoon and pat into an 8- or 9-inch pie pan. Bake at 350° for 8 minutes, and then set aside to cool.

When the South was quelled in the Civil War, condensed milk—then a new product—became popular as an inexpensive form of milk.
In Florida, this milk was used with good results as an ingredient for Key Lime Pie.

Pie Filling & Topping

- 1 14-OUNCE CAN SWEETENED CONDENSED MILK
- 3 EGGS (SEPARATED)
- 3 LIMES
- 1 CUP WHIPPING CREAM

Mix the milk and beaten egg yolks (reserve whites). Squeeze the limes into a separate bowl. Add lime juice to milk mixture. Whip the egg whites until stiff. Fold into milk mixture. Spoon into pie shell. Bake at 250° for 10 minutes. When cool, place in the refrigerator.

To serve, whip cream and spread on top of the pie. A little sugar and rum may be added to the cream if desired. This makes 6 servings.

Illinois Lincoln Thanksgiving Pumpkin Pie

Our family once drove from New York to Los Angeles in a secondhand Volkswagen bus. We camped out each night, all the way across the country. We were returning to Los Angeles with our three children, all under the age of ten, after two years of living in Rome. It was fun to be home again, and I was impressed with the nostalgic moods of the American camping sites. One of our overnight stops was in the New Salem State Park in Illinois There, we visited the small cabin where Abraham Lincoln and his family lived during his early adult years. It was here that the future president began studying law. This small town, on a wooded grove above the Sangamon River, has been restored for the nation to view. The visit left me feeling a bit closer to this great visionary president.

During the tragic times of the Civil War, President Lincoln heeded the letters of Mrs. Sarah Hale, who for twenty years had begged the government to declare Thanksgiving a legally "hallowed and exalted" day. Americans had always celebrated Thanksgiving, but it was not a national holiday until 1863 when President Lincoln proclaimed the last Thursday in November as a day of thanksgiving.

When we lived in Paris, I thought it would be fun to have a Thanksgiving dinner for our American student friends. In the street market on Rue Lepic, I purchased what I thought was a pumpkin and made a pie. Everyone was most impressed until they took a bite and found it tasted like soap. It was obvious that what I had bought was not a pumpkin but some bizarre kind of French squash. This recipe, though, is the classic pumpkin pie.

Illinois

"We have pumpkins at morning and pumpkins at noon. If it were not for pumpkins, we should be undone."

This poem reflects colonists' feelings about pumpkins. If it were not for pumpkins, colonial settlers might have starved. They ate them as vegetables, in soups, and for dessert (sweetened).

For basic piecrust recipe, see Washington Apple Pie on p. 80. For a single crust, use one-half ingredient amounts.

- 1 9-INCH UNBAKED PASTRY CRUST OF YOUR CHOICE (SEE SIDEBAR)
- 1½ CUPS CANNED OR FRESH COOKED, STRAINED PUMPKIN
- ¾ CUP HALF-AND-HALF
- 2 EGGS, BEATEN
- ⅔ CUP BROWN SUGAR
- ½ TEASPOON EACH GROUND GINGER, GROUND NUTMEG, AND SALT
- ¼ TEASPOON GROUND CLOVES
- FRESH WHIPPED CREAM (FOR TOPPING)

Combine ingredients (except piecrust and whipped cream) in a bowl. Blend well and pour into the piecrust. Bake at 400° for 55 minutes. Spoon whipped cream on top. This will serve 6.

Index